D0924355

*"This book is a must for young adults v
syndrome. Sue Levine and Brian Skotl
of experience and information-gatherin
resource for brothers a*

—David Tolleson, Executive Director, National Down Syndrome Congress

Fasten Your Seatbelt *is a compelling and essential resource for siblings, friends and family alike or for anyone interested in having a greater understanding of Down syndrome. If there is a more comprehensive or accessible guide to navigating the emotional pathways around Down Syndrome, I have yet to discover it.*

—Victoria Will, little sister to Jon Will, age 35

Fasten Your Seatbelt

a crash course on Down syndrome
for brothers and sisters

Brian G. Skotko & Susan P. Levine

Woodbine House   2009

Library of Congress Cataloging in Publication Data

Skotko, Brian.
  Fasten your seatbelt : a crash course on Down syndrome for brothers and sisters / Brian Skotko and Susan Levine. -- 1st ed.
    p. cm.
  Includes index.
  ISBN 978-1-890627-86-7
  1. Down syndrome--Juvenile literature. 2. Brothers and sisters--Juvenile literature. 3. People with mental disabilities--Juvenile literature. 4. Down syndrome--Patients--Family relationships--Juvenile literature. I. Levine, Susan P. II. Title.
  RC571.S56 2009
  616.85'8842--dc22   2008049753

Manufactured in the United States of America

10   9   8   7   6   5   4   3   2   1

DEDICATION

Brian dedicates this book to Kristin and Allison,
exceptional sisters with big hearts.

Sue dedicates this book to all the brothers and sisters she has met
through the years, and to her colleagues, Cheryl Gaudette and
Nancy Phalanukorn, whose dedication to the lives of children with
disabilities and their families has been a shared journey.

Sue and Brian would also like to thank our sibling advisors,
Andrew Cecchetti and Alison Herrington, who spent many hours
reviewing the manuscript. Their honest and thoughtful feedback
helped to make this book more complete.

Table of Contents

Introduction

One by one, brothers and sisters of all ages scribbled questions on blank index cards—no names attached!—and dropped them into a box in the center of the room. The doors were shut, and no parents were allowed in. As the program began, we pulled out those questions one at a time to discuss confidentially with the group. We were at a brothers-and-sisters conference, and everyone had come to discuss one thing—their sibling with Down syndrome.

For a combined 34 years, we have met more than 3,380 brothers and sisters at workshops like these around the country. Some attended programs sponsored by the National Down Syndrome Society or the National Down Syndrome Congress. Others shared their experiences with us at a sibling get-together sponsored by a local agency or Down syndrome group. Together, we answered some of the toughest and most challenging questions posed about brothers and sisters with Down syndrome.

What causes Down syndrome? If you have children one day, will they have Down syndrome? What should you do when people stare at your sister in public? How should you deal with people who use the "r" word? Where will your brother live when he gets older? These are just some of the many questions that were tossed into the box during these workshops.

In this book, we have gathered all of those thoughtful questions in one place, along with some answers. If you have been to one of our workshops, you might recognize your questions, presented here with no names attached. If you haven't been to a sibling group before, you probably have questions about your brother or sister that have been bugging you—maybe even one or two that you have been afraid to ask. If so, we hope you will find some helpful answers here. Every question deserves an answer, and every feeling is valid and important to explore.

Having a brother and sister with Down syndrome means you experience many joys and challenges. Let's start the discussion.

1 GEARING UP TO GO:

getting the facts about Down syndrome

You have probably already been asked by your friends, "So, what is Down syndrome?" Perhaps you offered an explanation about chromosomes that you learned from your science class. Maybe you mentioned some of the physical characteristics that are found among people with Down syndrome. You might have even talked about some of the ways in which your brother or sister is unique. But, have you ever felt like you needed more information yourself?

Sometimes when you are a brother or sister, you feel like you need to be the world's expert on Down syndrome. People will ask you lots of questions about the condition, probably for the rest of your life. When a friend comes over, he might want to know why they call it "Down syndrome." Perhaps during a trip to the mall, one of your friends might ask you if having a sister with Down syndrome means that you will have children with Down syndrome yourself one day. Even adults might want to know more about the medical conditions your brother or sister might face.

The purpose of this chapter is to give you the facts about Down syndrome. Included here are some of the most common questions that brothers and sisters across the country have asked—or have been asked by other people. After reading these answers, you will feel better prepared for the next time that someone wants to learn a little bit more about your brother or sister.

What causes Down syndrome?

There are three types of Down syndrome, all caused by having too many **chromosomes**—the microscopic packages of instructions in your body's cells that determine how you grow and develop. Every cell in your body has 46 of these chromosomes—23 that came from your father (originally from his sperm) and 23 that came from your mother (originally from her egg). Scientists number these chromosomes 1 through 22 and call the 23rd chromosome your "sex chromosome" because it determines whether you will be a boy or a girl. Typically, people have two copies of chromosome 1, two copies of chromosome 2, two copies of chromosome 3, and so on.

> There are three types of Down syndrome, all caused by having too many chromosomes—the microscopic packages of instructions in your body's cells that determine how you grow and develop.

As you might recall from your science classes, chromosomes contain **genes.** Some chromosomes are large and contain about 3,000 genes; others are small and have only about 200. A gene is a set of instructions that your body needs in order to work properly. For example, you have genes that tell your body what color your eyes should be. You have genes that determine how tall you will be. You also have genes that program your body to develop your heart, lungs, and liver. Scientists now believe that every person has approximately 25,000 genes!

TRISOMY 21

Approximately 95 percent of people with Down syndrome have three complete copies of chromosome 21 in every cell (and two copies of all the other chromosomes, just like you). This extra chromosome typically comes from the mother's egg before conception. As the cells divide and the baby continues to grow, this extra chromosome is copied along with all the others in every cell in the body. As a result, every cell in the body has one extra chromosome for a total of 47. This type of Down syndrome is called **"Trisomy 21."**

Chromosome 21 is one of the smallest chromosomes, containing approximately 200-400 genes. Since people with Down syndrome have an extra copy of chromosome 21, however, they have an extra set of the 200-400 genes that are on this chromosome in each of their cells. These extra genes result in many of the characteristics and medical conditions related to Down syndrome. Scientists are actively trying to figure out what each extra gene does in someone with Down syndrome.

TRANSLOCATION DOWN SYNDROME

Approximately 4 percent of people with Down syndrome have two copies of chromosome 21 and a third partial copy of chromosome 21 in their cells. In reality, this third copy is typically a combined copy of chromosome 14 and 21. Usually, the egg from the mother somehow manages to join parts of the 14th and 21st chromosomes into a single chromosome. In most cases, this recombination occurs before conception. After conception, this third copy develops in the baby as a chromosome 21 look-alike and is duplicated in every cell in the baby's body. This type of Down syndrome is called **"Translocation Down Syndrome."**

MOSAICISM

The last 1 percent of people with Down syndrome has a type called **"Mosaicism"** or **mosaic Down syndrome.** In this type, some of the body's cells have three copies of chromosome 21, whereas other cells have the typical two copies. This rare form of Down syndrome can occur because of a genetic change before or after conception. In some cases, the developing baby receives 3 copies of the 21st chromosome (just as in Trisomy 21, described above), but then manages to "lose" some of the third copies in developing cells. In other cases, the developing baby receives the typical 46 chromosomes from his or her parents. Then, shortly after conception, some of the duplicating cells acquire an extra chromosome, which leads to three copies of the 21st chromosome in certain cells.

The number and location of the cells in the body that have an extra chromosome 21 could determine how many characteristics and medical conditions someone with this type of Down syndrome might have. For example, if a lot of the cells in the heart have three copies of the chromosome 21, a person with mosaic Down syndrome might be more likely to have one of the heart conditions commonly associated with Down syndrome. If a lot of cells in the brain have three copies of chromosome 21, the person might experience more of the learning difficulties that are common to people with Down syndrome. Scientists are still trying to figure out how these few individuals with mosaic Down syndrome end up with three copies of chromosome 21 in only some of their cells.

In each of these three types of Down syndrome, what actually causes the extra chromosome to end up in the baby's cells?

That's a great question and scientists all over the world are trying to figure it out. Right now, we just don't know the answer. We do know that older women are more likely to have children with Down syndrome, so some people think that the chromosomes in a mother's eggs do not divide properly as a woman ages. However, this does not explain how babies with Down syndrome can be born to young mothers. Researchers don't currently have any other explanations other than a mother's age; some simply believe that the extra chromosome just randomly happens at times. Stay tuned, though, because researchers are certain to discover new clues soon.

How many people with Down syndrome are there?

One out of every 733 babies born in the United States has Down syndrome. This means that there are more than 400,000 people in the United States living with Down syndrome.

Is Down syndrome more common for boys or girls?

As far as researchers and scientists can tell, all three types of Down syndrome occur equally in boys and girls. Down syndrome occurs in people of all different races, religions, and ethnic origins.

> Down syndrome occurs in people of all different races, religions, and ethnic origins.

My friend said that kids get Down syndrome from the age of their parents. Is that true?

Scientists know that as mothers get older, the chances increase that their children will be born with Down syndrome (any of the three types). When a mother is 35 years old, for example, her chances of having a child with Down syndrome are approximately 1 in 353. This means that if there were 353 pregnant mothers, all of whom were aged 35, we would expect that one of them would have a child with Down syndrome.

When a mother is a bit older, say 40 years old, her chances of having a child with Down syndrome are approximately

1 in 85. This means that if there were 85 pregnant mothers, all of whom were aged 40, we would expect that one of them would have a child with Down syndrome. As you can see, it takes 353 mothers at the age of 35 to have one child with Down syndrome, whereas it takes only 85 mothers at the age of 40 to find one child with Down syndrome. Some scientists refer to this factor as "advanced maternal age," meaning that the older a mother is, the more likely it is that she might have a child with Down syndrome. However, scientists are not yet able to explain why older mothers are more likely to have babies with Down syndrome.

> Scientists know that as mothers get older, the chances increase that their children will be born with Down syndrome.

It is important to note, though, that a younger mother can still have a child with Down syndrome, even though her chance is lower than an older mother's. For example, a mother at age 26 has about a 1 in 1,285 chance of having a child with Down syndrome. More women, however, tend to have babies when they are younger, rather than older. So, just because there are more births in younger mothers, more babies with Down syndrome will be born to younger women.

And what about dads? Researchers are now beginning to believe that the age of the father might also affect the chances of having a child with Down syndrome. At the current time, however, it remains unclear how much of a role "advanced paternal age" plays.

Is Down syndrome contagious?

No. Neither you nor your friends will get Down syndrome by being around your brother or sister. If you are not born with Down syndrome, you cannot develop the condition.

If I have children one day, will they have Down syndrome?

You might have been asked by your friends—or you might be wondering yourself—about your chances of having a child with Down syndrome one day. The answer depends on the type of Down syndrome that your brother or sister has. If you are interested, you might ask your mother or father if they know your sibling's type of Down syndrome. If they do not know, this information can be obtained through genetic testing done by a doctor. The genetic testing usually involves taking a small amount of blood from your brother or sister to count the number of chromosomes in blood cells.

If your sibling has trisomy 21 or mosaic Down syndrome, you have the same chances of having a child with Down syndrome as anyone else in the world. Your brother or sister has no impact on your own chances of having a child with Down syndrome.

If your brother or sister has the very rare form of Down syndrome known as translocation Down syndrome, your chances are slightly increased if you are considered a "genetic carrier." A genetic carrier is someone who has the potential to pass a genetic condition on to their children without having the genetic condition themselves. Approximately one out of every two brothers and sisters who have a sibling with translocation Down syndrome is a genetic carrier. (A doctor can determine if you are one of these genetic carriers by analyzing a small amount of your blood.) If you are *not* a genetic carrier, your chances of having a child Down syndrome are the same as anyone else in the world. Your brother or sister has no impact on your own chances of having a child with Down syndrome.

If you are a genetic carrier, however, and you are a girl, your chances of having a child with Down syndrome can be as high as 15 percent. If you are a genetic carrier, and you are a boy, your chances can be as high as 5 percent. This means that if there were 100 adult sisters who were genetic carriers for transloca-tion Down syndrome, we would expect about 15 of them to have their own babies with translocation Down syndrome. If there were 100 adult brothers who were genetic carriers for transloca-tion Down syndrome, we would expect about 5 of them to have their own babies with translocation Down syndrome.

If your brother or sister has translocation Down syndrome, and you are interested in knowing if you are a "genetic carrier," talk with your parents. Perhaps they can arrange for you to have the necessary genetic testing. If not, you can always do this your-self when you are an adult, before you have your own children.

Why is it called "Down syndrome"?

Down syndrome is named after the doctor who first de-scribed it—John Langdon Down. Contrary to what some of your friends might think, the name has nothing to do with children feeling "down" or "depressed." However, the condition hasn't al-ways been known as "Down syndrome." How the name evolved is a story woven with science, advocacy, and passion.

John Langdon Down was a physician practicing in Lon-don, England, in the late nine-teenth century. After seeing lots of babies with similar physical characteristics, Dr. Down wanted to share his observations with other scientists. In 1862, he published a paper in a medical journal and described the common characteristics that we know chil-dren with Down syndrome have. We do not believe that Down syndrome first occurred at this time. (In fact, some pieces of art-work and historical data suggest that children might have had Down syndrome at least as early as the fifteenth century.) Dr. Down was simply the first person to appreciate the shared char-acteristics and describe Down syndrome for the first time.

> Down syndrome is named after the doctor who first described it—John Langdon Down.

He did not use the words "Down syndrome," however. He used the word "Mongolism," in reference to the similar facial characteristics that the children shared with people from Mongolia, a country in Asia positioned north of China. In 1961, nearly 100 years after Dr. Down first published his report, a group of doctors and genetic experts wrote to the editor of a medical journal that was publishing papers on the topic. The experts commented that the name was inaccurate and, at worst, not very sensitive to the people of Mongolia. They encouraged the editor to adopt a different name for the condition. The editor agreed and suggested "Down's Syndrome." In 1965, the World Health Organization, an important international health agency, confirmed the name, as well.

Advocates in the United States have since tweaked the name even more. An apostrophe is no longer used, and the word "syndrome" is spelled with a lower case "s." The official name is "Down syndrome." Since Dr. Down never had Down syndrome, himself, advocates and medical professionals did not feel the name should be possessive. (This is in contrast to other medical conditions, such as Lou Gehrig's Disease, where the person it is named after actually had the named condition.) In 1974, the National Institutes of Health, an important governmental health agency, formally discouraged the use of the apostrophe for conditions like Down syndrome. You might notice, however, that people in some other countries still use the name "Down's Syndrome."

"Mongolism," the original description for Down syndrome, is now considered to be an offensive word and is labeled so by many dictionaries. Going forward, we will refer to it as the "M" word. Regrettably, there are still people today—including doctors—who continue to use the term, sometimes knowingly but oftentimes unknowingly, in reference to people with Down syndrome. Now that you know the history of the word, if you ever hear people using it, you can update them with more accurate and appropriate terminology.

What is the best way to write or talk about people with Down syndrome?

Have you ever heard people say anything along these lines?
- "That *Down's girl* is so cute."
- "*Down syndrome kids* are really nice."
- "My *Down syndrome child* is making great progress in school."

At first glance, the sentences actually seem rather complimentary—who wouldn't want to be cute, nice, or doing well in school? However, many advocates suggest there are better ways to phrase the italicized words in the sentences above. When the word "Down syndrome" comes before the other words—"girl," "kids," "child"—it seems like a certain breed of humans exist: the Down syndrome people.

But, you know that Down syndrome doesn't define your sister or brother. They are talented people who play musical instruments, go to school, hold jobs. They are first and foremost people like the rest of us. So, advocates recommend that we say "people with Down syndrome," to emphasize that they are "people first" who just happen to have Down syndrome. Let's try rewriting the sentences above:
- "That *girl with Down syndrome* is cute."
- "*Kids with Down syndrome* are really nice."
- "My *child with Down syndrome* is making great progress in school."

Did you notice the difference? Now, the sentences are all about the girl, the kids, and the child. Down syndrome is a descriptor, not the most important part. The distinction might seem subtle, but for many people with Down syndrome, the difference is very important. This is called "People First" language, and also applies to people with other disabilities. For example,

How you describe your brother or sister with Down syndrome will set the stage for how other people view him or her.

advocates recommend saying "man with cerebral palsy," "girl with autism," or "daughter who is blind."

You can make a big difference just by choosing the words that you use and modeling sensitivity to people with Down syndrome. How you describe your brother or sister with Down syndrome will set the stage for how other people view him or her.

How can you tell if someone has Down syndrome?

People with Down syndrome have several shared physical characteristics. Among the most common features that you might have noticed in your own brother or sister are the following:

- *hypotonia*: weak muscle tone (making the muscles seem somewhat "floppy"), especially in babies
- *hyperflexibility*: the ability to bend arms and legs further than usual and sometimes in different directions
- *flat nasal bridge*: a flattened area at the top of the nose
- *oblique palpebral fissures*: the outside corners of the eyes point upwards, rather than horizontally
- *epicanthal folds*: extra skin folds at the corners of the eyes near the nose
- *small head*
- *short neck*, often with extra skin at the back of the neck
- *small mouth*, sometimes with the tongue sticking forward or protruding
- *small ears*

- *single transverse palmar crease*: a single crease in the middle of the palm of the hand, rather than two or three
- *short fifth finger:* shorter than typical pinky fingers, and oftentimes curved inward
- *wide space between first and second toes*
- *Brushfield spots*: white or yellow speckles in the colored part (iris) of the eye

Not all people with Down syndrome have all of these characteristics, but some do. Just in case you were wondering, a person without Down syndrome might have one or more of the characteristics listed here, too. For example, you or someone else in your family or school might have a single palmar crease or a curved pinky finger. This does not mean the person has Down syndrome! People with Down syndrome are just more likely to have some of these characteristics.

In order to be sure of the diagnosis a doctor will order a "karyotype," which is a blood test that will determine the number of chromosomes the baby has.

If a doctor suspects that a new baby might have Down syndrome, he or she will look for these above features. The more features that a baby has, the more likely he or she might have Down syndrome. In order to be sure of the diagnosis, however, a doctor will order a "karyotype," which is a blood test that will determine the number of chromosomes the baby has. With a karyotype, a doctor will be able to know, with certainty, if a baby has Down syndrome and what type of Down syndrome he or she has.

With the advances in science, doctors can now determine if a baby has Down syndrome before he is born. This is called a "prenatal diagnosis." By passing a needle through a mother's womb through a process called "amniocentesis" or "chorionic villus sampling," a physician can get a sample of tissue or fluid and do a karyotype to determine how many chromosomes a baby has. It is a mother's decision as to whether she would like to have such a test done while she is pregnant.

Will my brother always stick out his tongue?

Babies with Down syndrome often stick out their tongues for two reasons:
1. Their mouths tend to be smaller, so there is less space for the tongue. By sticking out their tongues, babies create more open mouth space to breathe.
2. Babies with Down syndrome often have weak muscles. Since the tongue is a muscle, they might have less control over its movements.

As children get older, their mouths will become bigger, and their muscle strength will improve. Babies who originally stuck out their tongues will usually begin to keep their tongues in their mouths. If your brother continues to keep his tongue out, your parents might take him to see an occupational or speech therapist. These are specialists who can work on exercises to strengthen the tongue's muscles as well as the muscles of the lips and face.

Why are kids with Down syndrome "floppy" at birth and then "strong" later on?

You are right that babies with Down syndrome frequently have "hypotonia," a condition that means their muscles are still weak and not yet coordinated. This often gives the appearance that a baby is "floppy."

Some children with Down syndrome also have "hyperflexibility," meaning that they are able to bend their joints in all sorts of directions. For example, they may be able to put one foot behind their head when they are sitting on the floor.

Our bones are connected to each other with tissues called "ligaments." Children who are hyperflexible have ligaments that are loose—or "lax." Doctors often refer to this condition as "ligamentous laxity." Children who have this condition may seem like they can wiggle out of any hug or squirm out of the tightest hold.

Physical therapists—or "PTs" for short—are specialists who are trained to help

Physical therapists—or "PTs" for short—are specialists who are trained to help children with Down syndrome strengthen muscles.

children with Down syndrome strengthen these muscles. They have a whole series of exercises that they use for babies and children of all ages to help them get stronger, reaching milestones like sitting, crawling, and walking.

If you have a brother or sister with Down syndrome who is older than about 5, you might know that, at times, they can be incredibly "strong." Have you ever been in a mall when your sister has a temper tantrum, decides to sit down, and no one is able to move her? Or, does your brother ever refuse to give up the television remote, and no one is able to free it from his clutch?

Researchers do not yet know what is happening in the muscles of older children and young adults with Down syndrome that make them appear to be so strong in these situations. Expert physical therapists believe that, in these moments, people with Down syndrome have learned to use all of their weight to move their bodies or to hang onto something with all of their might! This behavior can look like stubbornness, but it more likely a sign that the person is feeling frustrated or annoyed.

What medical problems go along with Down syndrome?

Every person with Down syndrome is different. Some people have many medical conditions, whereas others have seemingly few. Currently, there is no way to anticipate which medical con-

Currently, there is no way to anticipate which medical conditions a baby with Down syndrome might have as he or she grows up. ...ditions a baby with Down syndrome might have as he or she grows up. We will briefly talk about some of the medical conditions that are common to people with Down syndrome, but remember that your brother or sister will most likely not have all of these conditions.

NEWBORNS

When babies are born with Down syndrome, about half of them have some heart condition that will require medical attention. Many of these newborns will need to have surgery in order to correct the heart defects, but because of advances in science and technology, the surgical correction is now very successful. Newborns with Down syndrome also tend to have difficulties learning how to feed, so some may have trouble gaining weight. Some might have constipation, and others might require surgical correction if their intestines are not structured properly. In addition, some newborns have hearing loss or eye problems.

INFANTS

As babies get a bit older, their doctors will begin to look for signs of ear infections and hearing difficulties. Additionally, babies with Down syndrome will have their thyroid glands tested. The thyroid gland is located in your neck and produces hormones that are important for regulating many things in your body, including your sense of temperature and your digestion. Many babies with Down syndrome have thyroid glands that do not produce enough hormones and need medications to make up for the lost hormones.

Very rarely, babies with Down syndrome can develop "infantile spasms" or "tonic-clonic seizures," two conditions in which extra electrical activity in a baby's brain causes some unusual body movements, such as stiffening, staring, or jerking. Frequently, babies who experience these shaking episodes see a *neurologist*—that is, a doctor who specializes in the brain. There are many medications that can help control seizures.

CHILDREN

Between the ages of 2 and 5, many children with Down syndrome need to start wearing glasses to help them see clearly. Beginning around this age period, you might also notice that your brother or sister snores or has trouble sleeping. Your sibling might even have "sleep apnea," a condition in which he does not get enough oxygen when he sleeps, sometimes resulting in brief moments where children stop breathing altogether. At this age, sleep apnea is often related to enlarged tonsils in a mouth that is already smaller compared to children without Down syndrome. In such cases, your mother or father might take your sibling to see a doctor called an otolaryngologist (pronounced otto-laren-GALL-e-jist), or an "ENT," someone who specializes in the "ears, nose, and throat." Children with Down syndrome should also continue to have their ears checked for ear infections.

Around the age of 2, your brother or sister should be checked for celiac disease. This is a condition where your body does not properly digest foods containing wheat, barley, rye, and sometimes oats. This can result in diarrhea, stomach bloating, weight loss, and poor growth. Some research suggests that as many as 16 out of every 100 people with Down syndrome might have this condition. If your brother or sister has celiac disease, he or she will be prescribed a special diet, avoiding foods that contain barley, wheat, rye, and sometimes oats. This might mean that your whole family will need to help out by not buying such foods at the grocery store. At a minimum, you will need to be careful not to leave these sorts of foods where your brother might grab and eat them.

You might have heard that children with Down syndrome have a higher chance of developing leukemia, a type of blood cancer. While this is true, the chance of a child with Down syndrome developing leukemia is still very low: only 1 in every

100 children with Down syndrome will develop leukemia. Fortunately, children with Down syndrome respond very well to medical treatment, and most can now expect a full recovery.

In addition to having Down syndrome, some children can also have other conditions that affect their ability to learn. Learning disabilities such as autism (which causes problems with social skills and communication) or AD/HD (which causes difficulty with attention and behavior control) might also be diagnosed around the time your sibling reaches school age.

Children with Down syndrome between the ages of 5 and 13 can continue to have many of the medical issues already mentioned. Frequently, people with Down syndrome also experience some dry skin that might require some extra care.

ADOLESCENTS

One of the most common medical conditions among adolescents with Down syndrome is obesity. This results from a combination of influences. One reason is that people with Down syndrome do not burn calories as quickly as other people do. Another reason is that many young adults with Down syndrome do not have the same athletic and social opportunities that promote good fitness. Adolescents with Down syndrome who have weight problems often benefit from meeting with a *dietitian*, a specialist who can help teach their parents and them about proper nutrition and making healthy food choices.

Just like other overweight teens, young adults with Down syndrome can also develop diabetes, a condition where your body is not able to store sugar that can be used for energy. Teens with Down syndrome and diabetes would benefit from seeing an *endocrinologist*—a physician who can help prescribe medicine to manage this condition

Overweight teens can also develop "sleep apnea," as discussed in the section on "Children" above. At this age, the breathing problems are often caused by excess weight pressing on the throat, but apnea can still be related to untreated tonsil enlargement. Sometimes, teens with Down syndrome who have sleep apnea require a special machine to help them breathe better while they are sleeping.

Young adults with Down syndrome, especially those born with heart conditions, should continue to have their hearts examined, as new cardiac conditions can arise during adolescence. Many teens might also have missing, small, or misshapen teeth. Seeing a dentist on a regular basis can be of great help.

Just like everyone else, young adults with Down syndrome can also develop emotional problems, including depression (where they feel sad a lot; for example, never quite recovering from the loss of a much loved grandpa) or obsessive-compulsive disorder (where they worry excessively about details; for example, constantly cleaning their hands because they believe that they are dirty even though they are not).

ADULTS

Around the age of 20, some adults with Down syndrome develop seizures for the first time. During a seizure, the electrical activity in a person's brain causes unusual and uncontrollable body movements including staring, head drops, or jerking. About 8 out of every 100 people with Down syndrome will develop a seizure condition at some point in their life, but many adults benefit from medications prescribed by a neurologist.

Also, since the joints of adults with Down syndrome can sometimes be looser, your adult brother or sister might develop some knee problems. An *orthopedist*, a doctor who specializes in bones and the ligaments that connect them, can help address these concerns.

It is important for adults with Down syndrome to have good skin care. Sometimes the skin is rough and dry (*xerosis*), very thick (*hyperkeratosis*), or cracked and scaly, especially around the mouth (*cheilitis*). Applying lotions and creams on a regular basis in addition to seeing a *dermatologist*—or skin doctor—might be important for adults with these conditions.

Finally, like other people, adults with Down syndrome may develop memory problems as they grow older. Most often these problems are due to treatable conditions such as depression, anxiety, or chronic pain. However, like other adults, they can also develop Alzheimer disease, a condition where older people become increasingly confused, forgetful, and disoriented. It is a progressive form of memory loss—meaning that people who have the condition can slowly forget some basic tasks such as how to choose clothes for themselves, what the names of family members are, how to function on a job, and how to get around in their own homes.

People with Down syndrome can develop Alzheimer disease in their 40s and 50s, some 10 to 20 years earlier than people without Down syndrome. Because of this reality, many scientists have been studying the link between the two conditions. Researchers are beginning to discover that many of the genes that cause Alzheimer disease are located on the 21st chromosome. Since people with Down syndrome typically have an extra copy of this chromosome, they might have an overabundance of certain genes, causing an earlier onset of the memory loss. Fortunately, there are many new medications to help people with Alzheimer disease, and adults with Down syndrome are benefiting from them.

Adults with Down syndrome are less likely to develop breast cancer, lung cancer, mouth cancer, and other cancers when compared to people who don't have Down syndrome.

On the flip side, having an extra chromosome might protect adults with Down syndrome from developing certain cancers. Did you know that adults with Down syndrome are less likely to develop breast cancer, lung cancer, mouth cancer, and other cancers when compared to people who don't have Down syndrome? Some scientists believe that there are some good genes on the 21st chromosome, and that by having an extra copy, people with Down syndrome have added protection. For this reason, some researchers feel that adults with Down syndrome might hold some of the keys to treating cancers. If scientists could figure out which genes are beneficial when there is an extra copy on the additional 21st chromosome, they could try to create the proteins made by these genes in a laboratory. Theoretically, these products could then be given to people without Down syndrome to prevent certain cancers.

As always, if you have questions about the medical conditions that your brother or sister might have, consider asking your parents for more information. You might also ask if you can accompany your sibling on his next doctor's visit so that you can ask the physician some of your own questions, either in front of your sibling or in private. You could also ask your parents to mention your concerns to the doctor and let them get back to you with the answers.

How long do people with Down syndrome live?

Due to advances in science and medicine, people with Down syndrome are now living longer than they ever have before. Back in 1983, the average person with Down syndrome lived to only 25 years old, primarily because of heart complications. Now, the average person with Down syndrome in the U.S. can expect to live to nearly 60 years old. According to some reports, approximately 12 out of 100 adults with Down syndrome will even live to 70 years old. This means that people with Down syndrome are now approaching a normal lifespan, as the average person living in the United States can now expect to live 78 years.

How can one extra chromosome make people so different?

Excellent question! In fact, researchers across the country—and the world—are trying to figure this out. We know that

Researchers are trying to discover, right now, how the 21st chromosome makes people with Down syndrome who they are.

most people with Down syndrome have an extra copy of the 21st chromosome, but researchers believe that some genes on the 21st chromosome cause greater changes than others when there are three copies. Scientists are now asking the following questions:

- Is there a gene on the 21st chromosome that, when triplicated, results in the heart problems seen in people who have Down syndrome? Similarly, is there a gene that, when there is an extra copy, results in thyroid problems in people with Down syndrome?
- What about finding genes that control some of the learning challenges?
- Or the genes that seem to contribute to the early aging process?

The list of questions can go on and on, but researchers are trying to discover, right now, how the 21st chromosome makes people with Down syndrome who they are. Someday in the future, researchers are hoping that they might be able to figure out how to "turn off" the extra 21st chromosome or, at least, try to block the effects of the genes on that chromosome that are causing the most problems. If you are interested in finding out more about the latest research, check out some of the resources in Chapter 9.

SUMMARY POINTS

- There are three types of Down syndrome—trisomy 21, translocation Down syndrome, and mosaic Down syndrome—all caused by having too many chromosomes, the packages of instructions for your body.
- Down syndrome occurs in people of all races, religions, and ethnic origins.
- One in every 733 babies born in the United States has Down syndrome.
- If your sibling has trisomy 21 or mosaic Down syndrome, your chances of having a child with Down syndrome are the same as anyone else in the world. If, however, your sibling has translocation Down syndrome, your chances of having a child with Down syndrome are greater if you are a genetic carrier.
- Currently, there is no way to anticipate which medical conditions a baby with Down syndrome might have as he or she grows up. Regular medical checkups help your brother or sister to stay healthy, because any concerns that might develop can be identified and treated early.
- Researchers are trying to discover, right now, how the 21st chromosome makes people with Down syndrome who they are.

2 ROAD TEST :
how people with Down syndrome learn

More than ever before, people with Down syndrome are having great success in classrooms across the country. However, there are many different types of school settings for people with learning differences. One style of learning does not fit all. Your brother or sister with Down syndrome might be in a classroom with people who do not have disabilities for most of the day, or he or she might be in a classroom specially designed for students with disabilities. Perhaps, your brother or sister is home-schooled. Or, maybe, he or she has finished high school and is taking classes in a postsecondary education program.

One style of learning does not fit all.

You might have also noticed that people with Down syndrome vary greatly in their learning abilities. Some students seem to keep up in the classroom without too much trouble and have good social and communication skills. Other students seem to have many learning challenges, including difficulty with speech and problems with behavior.

The purpose of this chapter is to help explain the range of abilities in people with Down syndrome and what is possible in today's classrooms. Just like you, your brother or sister will never stop learning, regardless of his or her ability level. After reading this chapter, you will be able to understand what your parents and teachers consider when trying to decide on the best educational options for your brother or sister.

Why does it take people with Down syndrome longer to learn things?

The honest answer is that we do not know. As we discussed in Chapter 1, people with Down syndrome typically have an extra copy of the 21st chromosome. Somehow, having an extra set of all of the genes that are on this chromosome makes it harder for people with Down syndrome to learn things that might come easily to you.

Perhaps you have heard of an IQ test. This is an exam, often given by a psychologist or learning specialist, that tries to measure how smart a person is. IQ tests usually require the person to have good communication skills to respond. As you probably know, Down syndrome almost always causes some delays in speech skills, so this puts children with Down syndrome at a disadvantage when they are trying to show what they know! Nonetheless, most people with Down syndrome will have some degree of intellectual disability or "mental retardation," as some physicians say. You should know, however, that having an intellectual disability does not mean someone is incapable of learning. Rather, it means that people with Down syndrome tend to learn more slowly than other kids their age and need more practice before they understand.

Having an intellectual disability does not mean someone is incapable of learning.

You undoubtedly know that people without disabilities have different academic strengths—for example, maybe you are really good at social studies, but your friend is a wizard at math. The same is true of people with Down syndrome. Some students with Down syndrome learn quickly; others might take a very long time to learn even basic concepts in school. There is a great variation in learning abilities, but currently, there is no way for doctors or teachers to tell which babies with Down syndrome will grow up to be the faster learners. As you might know, some people with Down syndrome also have other medical conditions such as hearing loss, autism, or behavioral problems that can affect how easily they learn.

The goal for all students with Down syndrome, however, remains the same: to help them to become the most talented and educated people that they are capable of becoming. As we will discuss later in this chapter, reaching this goal requires work on the part of parents, teachers, and people with Down syndrome themselves.

Are some subjects in school harder or easier for people with Down syndrome?

People with Down syndrome like all sorts of subjects in school. You might have noticed that your brother or sister has a favorite: music, science, art, or maybe reading? Regardless of their preferences, however, students with Down syndrome will frequently find certain aspects of school challenging:

- Oftentimes, math, reading, and writing can be challenging activities for students with Down syndrome. In a social studies class, for example, your sister might need someone to help her read and understand the textbooks. In science, your brother might use a calculator to compute the results of a classroom experiment. For an English lesson, your sister might turn to a classroom aide for help in writing a short essay.

- People with Down syndrome sometimes have trouble remembering lots of facts. Your sister, for example, might find it difficult to memorize simple addition problems (like 2 + 8) or to recall all of the thirteen colonies. On the other hand, she might be really good at learning *how* to do something. She might easily pick up how to make a collage in art class or quickly learn how to play a game at recess. Teachers should recognize that students with Down syndrome often have trouble remembering facts—a type of memory called "declarative memory"—and should be making accommodations (or changes) in the classroom to help your brother or sister. For example, the teacher might repeat lessons frequently or make pictures or other visual aids to help your sibling master some facts.

- Students with Down syndrome can also have difficulties with abstract concepts. Understanding a lesson on "democracy" in history class might be challenging. Counting money in math class and then figuring out how much change they should get when buying lunch could be tough. Discussing qualities like pitch and melody in a music class could be confusing. Good teachers realize that most people with Down syndrome learn best when lessons are more concrete and visual. Breaking down abstract reasoning into a series of short, real-life examples with visual aids or pictures can frequently help students with Down syndrome begin to understand bigger concepts. For example, a lesson on democracy might start with practicing on a mock voting booth. Students could learn money concepts by using a calculator to buy some toys in a classroom store. And, finally, a lesson on melody and pitch might start by playing some popular songs and deciding whether they are "happy" or "sad" songs by pointing to happy or sad faces on a poster board.

> Good teachers realize that most people with Down syndrome learn best when lessons are more concrete and visual.

- Students with Down syndrome tend to learn better when they are shown *how* to do things rather than just being told what to do. Following a direction using only listening skills can be harder than following along and seeing how to do it (using both visual skills and listening skills). Also, to keep children focused in the classroom, teachers sometimes use picture charts to help remind them of the routine or what to do next. You might know exactly what to do in the classroom after you've finished your seat work, but a student with Down syndrome might forget. The picture chart can be a perfect way to remind him or her of the right thing to do.

■ Finally, some students with Down syndrome find it challenging, at times, to stay focused. Something might seem really interesting for a few minutes, and then they are ready for something new! Teachers and aides can use several strategies for keeping such students engaged. One technique might be pairing the student with another classmate so that they can work together and not become so quickly bored. Or teachers may use more visual aids than usual or provide more opportunities for hands-on learning.

In contrast, some subjects in school might be easier for someone with Down syndrome:

■ Does your brother or sister like to listen to music or watch movies with lots of songs? Some people with Down syndrome have a natural ability to appreciate music, and some researchers have found that they have a normal sense of rhythm and timing. Because of this, people with Down syndrome can be extremely motivated to participate in music class.

■ People with Down syndrome might also do well in art class, where they can explore their creative skills and express deep emotions. Some students with Down syndrome really excel with painting and drawing.

■ Some children with Down syndrome love to read! In fact, some experts actually recommend trying to teach children with Down syndrome to read at an early age to help them with communication skills. Although your brother or sister may struggle to understand the abstract concepts in science or social studies textbooks, he or she may read fictional stories very easily. In fact, some people with Down syndrome can actually read on a high-school level by the time they are young adults, according to new research.

- Spelling might also be a favorite for your brother or sister. In fact, you might have noticed that your sibling can be your best spellchecker. For reasons still unknown, some students with Down syndrome have an easy time with spelling.

How hard or easy a class is for your brother or sister will ultimately have as much to do with the classroom teaching as with your sibling's ability. Creative teachers, appropriate accommodations, and good communication between your parents and the school will all help in making the various subjects more understandable for your brother or sister.

Why is learning to talk so hard?

Let's start by looking at the way babies normally begin to talk. First, most babies without Down syndrome begin to babble when they are about six months old. Babies typically use "Mama" and "Dada" with meaning around the age of one, and develop a vocabulary of at least 4 to 10 words when they are about one and a half years old. Between the ages of two and three, children begin putting words together in a meaningful way, and after that, they use longer phrases and sentences.

Babies with Down syndrome go through all of these same stages, just at a slower pace. As we discussed in Chapter 1, infants with Down syndrome often have smaller mouths and less control of their tongues. Because of this, learning to talk can sometimes be challenging.

Many parents teach their children with Down syndrome to communicate with hand gestures before they are ready to speak.

This does not mean that babies and children with Down syndrome have trouble communicating. Talking is just one part of communication. We also communicate with our eyes, gestures, and "body language." Can you tell if your mom is mad even if she doesn't say anything? Or, you probably know when your friend is upset even if he never mentions it. You know that people communicate a lot of emotions and thoughts in ways other than talking. So, too, do babies and children with Down syndrome.

Many parents teach their children with Down syndrome to communicate with hand gestures before they are ready to speak. Many researchers believe that children with Down syndrome have a lot they want to say, but they just haven't developed the ability to form the words. So, in the meantime, using signs or gestures can help.

The signs or gestures that are taught are usually borrowed from American Sign Language (ASL), which is an actual language used by people who are deaf or hard of hearing. Since the gestures used with children with Down syndrome are just a small piece of this form of communication, it is probably better to say that a child uses signs or gestures, rather than saying that they speak in "sign language." Also, the sign is always taught with the spoken word.

Some common signs taught to children with Down syndrome are:

- *yes*: Make a fist with your right hand and then roll your wrist forward
- *more*: Bring all of your fingertips together on each hand, facing each other. Bring your hands together until they are touching.
- *eat*: Start by bringing all of your fingertips together on your right hand, starting with that hand extended away from your body facing your face. Bring your fingers to your mouth.

- *drink*: Form your right hand around an imaginary cup, bringing it to your lips as though you were taking a drink.

You might be wondering: if children learn to communicate with sign gestures, will they be less likely to talk one day? The answer is no. Family and friends will continue to talk to babies and children with Down syndrome, encouraging speech. The gestures are meant to be a way for children with Down syndrome to express themselves while waiting for them to learn to talk. As they develop their speech, the gestures are slowly dropped.

Many children with Down syndrome also see *speech and language therapists,* professionals who are trained to help children learn how to speak. These therapists might work on strengthening children's tongues or teaching them how to properly form certain words. They can also help children learn how to pronounce difficult sounds, and they can work on enunciation—that is, how to speak clearly so everyone can understand.

Even after they have developed speech, many children and young adults with Down syndrome continue to need some help from speech therapists. Some people with Down syndrome stutter, and others continue to have trouble making certain sounds clearly. Researchers aren't sure why, but it's also usually harder for children with Down syndrome to learn grammar and other language rules. Speech therapists are trained to help with all of these issues.

Lastly, there is a small percentage of children with Down syndrome who never learn to speak. Researchers do not yet know why some children are unable to form words. We do know that these children will still be able to communicate through other methods. For example, some of these children learn to communicate by pointing to or arranging a series of pictures, and others learn to use high-tech voice synthesizers or other communication devices. Still others continue to use sign gestures along with verbalizations to get their thoughts and emotions across.

Why did my brother repeat a grade?

Your parents most likely work very closely with your brother's teachers in setting his academic goals. They all work to help your brother learn as much as he possibly can. Sometimes, this means that it would actually be more helpful for your brother to repeat a grade than to advance to the next year where he might be way over his head.

> Children with Down syndrome usually take extra time in learning new things.

Children with Down syndrome usually take extra time in learning new things. If parents and teachers feel that a student has not gained all of the skills needed to do well in the next grade, often they will spend a repeat year trying to reinforce some of these necessary skills.

Children with Down syndrome might also repeat a year if their teachers and parents think they need to master more social, emotional, or self-help skills before moving on to the next grade. For instance, a kindergartener might still be having trouble paying attention to the teacher, sitting still at circle time, and following instructions at the end of the year. His parents and teachers might decide he needs to master these skills before moving on to first grade, where it is even more important to follow classroom rules.

Repeating a grade should not be viewed as a failure. Instead, think about it as a carefully thought-out plan by your parents and your brother's teachers to best prepare him for the future.

What is the best way to educate my sister with Down syndrome?

Since students with Down syndrome have varying levels of needs and talents, there is no one "right way" to provide an education for them. Some students with Down syndrome find suc-

Children with Down syndrome often have more academic success when they learn in inclusion classrooms.

cess by being included in "regular classrooms"; others maximize their potential in classrooms designed for students with learning disabil-ities. Still other children with Down syndrome learn best when they are home schooled. Let's begin by discussing the advan-tages and disadvantages of each option.

INCLUSION

Some students with Down syndrome attend the same classes that students without disabilities take. This education-al model is called "inclusion" because people with disabilities are "included" in the regular classrooms. Another term that is sometimes used is "mainstreaming." One of the advantages of inclusion is that people with Down syndrome can develop friendships with classmates who don't have disabilities. They can also pick up some social and behavior skills from their classmates without disabilities. By helping them feel "includ-ed," this model emphasizes that they are more alike than unlike other people their age.

Many researchers have demonstrated that children with Down syndrome often have more academic success when they learn in inclusion classrooms. According to these education ex-perts, people with Down syndrome also have better chances at getting jobs when they are older if they were educated with the inclusion model.

Some critics argue that having someone with Down syn-drome in the classroom will slow everyone else down. Research has shown that this is not true, provided inclusion is done cor-rectly. In fact, education experts have demonstrated that stu-dents without disabilities get a better education when someone with a disability is in their classroom. One reason is that when inclusion is done correctly, additional teachers or aides are present in the classroom, which gives every student more opportunities to interact with an educator. In addition, the classmates without disabilities have been shown to have emotional, social, and self-esteem benefits. In short, people with Down syndrome often have a positive impact!

Inclusion, however, is only successful if everyone is committed to it, including your sister, your parents, your sister's teacher, and the school administration. One of the big disadvantages of inclusion is that often all of the needed supports are not in place. As you probably know, you just can't push your sister into a classroom and expect her to succeed. She needs accommodations, such as a personal aide, extra time on tests, or modified homework. Especially in middle or high school, she may also need an extra teacher to "co-teach" some or all of her classes, adapting instruction and material to her level and learning style.

If the supports your sister needs are not available, she might be set up for failure, and find the curriculum too hard, the work too much, and the topics too challenging. In addition, to cut costs, schools often include too many students with disabilities in one classroom. Sometimes, this makes too much work for the teacher, who needs to prepare individualized accommodations and class work for each of the students, thereby reducing the amount of attention each student receives. The art of making inclusion work is providing the right amount of support that your sister needs to find success in a regular classroom.

One other disadvantage that families sometimes mention is teasing. You know that kids can sometimes be cruel and may pick on students with Down syndrome or other disabilities. Additionally, some people with Down syndrome mention that they have a tough time keeping friends. Yes, the classmates might be nice, but do they phone your sister after school like they do their other friends? And, when they graduate and go to different high schools or colleges, will they still be your sister's friends? We attempt to answer some of these tough questions in Chapter 6.

SEPARATE SPECIAL EDUCATION CLASSES

Some people with Down syndrome attend classrooms only with students who have learning or behavioral disabilities. In these classrooms, they may work on the general education curriculum, or they may work on a separate curriculum, perhaps with a greater attention to "functional skills" such as basic reading skills, money handling, grooming, or job readiness. Often, these classrooms are smaller, containing about 6-15 students with one teacher and one or two assistants (or "aides").

You probably know where the special education classes are located in your school. You might have noticed children with Down syndrome (maybe your sister!) and other disabilities in those classrooms.

Some students with Down syndrome go to an entirely separate school with only special education classrooms. These very specialized schools might use different teaching methods or slow down the instruction even more to help students with greater learning challenges. This type of placement usually occurs when parents feel that the local school cannot handle all of the student's needs. For this type of placement, students often have to travel further than they would have if they were attending their local school.

Separate smaller classes may be appropriate for children who cannot focus their attention or become over-stimulated in larger, busier classrooms.

One of the advantages of separate classes is that some students with Down syndrome can learn at a pace that is more in line with their development. The teacher can speed up or slow down depending on how fast the students are learning. They might also use special techniques or technology to teach reading and math skills to students with learning disabilities. Another advantage, often mentioned by parents, is that their children develop long-term relationships with some classmates, bonds that stretch beyond the classroom into Special Olympics and other social settings. These separate smaller classes may also be appropriate for children who cannot focus their attention or become over-stimulated in larger, busier classrooms.

One of the disadvantages of this option is that there may be fewer opportunities to interact with peers who do not have disabilities. The students with disabilities have their own classrooms, and they may also have their own lunch table and recess time. Critics argue that these students are missing the opportunity to build social relationships with people who don't have disabilities and to learn important social skills in the process. Critics also object that students with Down syndrome are not being academically pushed as much. The lesson plans often move at a slower pace, and there may not be clear-cut learning objectives for the class, like there are for students studying the typical curriculum.

HOME SCHOOL

Some students with Down syndrome stay at home, and their mom or dad serves as their teacher during the day. This is called "home schooling" because the students go to school at home. Families who choose this option cite any number of reasons for doing so: dissatisfaction with the schools in the local area, the desire to teach their own children, a belief that children learn best in the home environment, an opportunity to individually tailor the lessons to their child's needs, working at the pace set by the student.

One advantage of home schooling for students with Down syndrome is that they can advance as soon as they learn a topic. A student's mother or father can go as quickly or as slowly as the person with Down syndrome needs. Additionally, many supporters of home schooling believe that no one knows a child as well as his or her mother or father. They might be able to identi-

> One advantage of home schooling for students with Down syndrome is that they can advance as soon as they learn a topic.

fy their child's weaknesses more accurately and tailor strategies to strengthen their academic skills.

One disadvantage of home schooling can be the lack of social interactions with other children with and without disabilities. Many children who are homeschooled do interact with other homeschooled students, but critics claim that the encounters are less frequent than those in inclusion or special education classrooms. The student with Down syndrome might have fewer opportunities to develop friendships or work on his or her social skills.

COMBINATION

Some students with Down syndrome are educated through a combination of the above three ways. For example, your sister might be in inclusion classrooms for subjects like music, art, and social studies, but attend special education classes for math and reading. Your sister might also be homeschooled for grade school, but then your parents might decide to send her to special education classes or inclusion classes for high school to maximize social opportunities. By working with teachers and school administrators, your parents can create a mix of these educational systems to meet your sister's needs.

All three educational systems have advantages and disadvantages. Deciding whether inclusion, special education, homeschooling, or some combination is best for your sister is a decision that your parents and your sister's teachers must carefully consider. If you have additional questions about your sister's classes, consider asking your parents why they chose a particular plan for your sister.

Does inclusion just apply to schools?

Out in the community, there are many inclusive activities that your brother might choose to get involved in. When it comes to sports, for example, your brother might play on a local soccer team that is composed primarily of people without disabilities.

This is the practice of "inclusion" on the sports field. Alternatively, your brother might play basketball on the weekends with a Special Olympics team that is composed only of athletes with disabilities. In many ways, this mirrors the "separate special education classroom" model.

Neither one of these types of teams is necessarily the "right" or "best" option for any given person with Down syndrome. It depends on the purpose of the activity, as well as on your brother's own wishes. For example, if the purpose is for your brother to get the maximum amount of playing time and to increase his self-esteem by making lots of goals, then playing on the Special Olympics team would likely be the better option. Or, if the purpose is for him to play with his friends from school and develop his social skills, then playing on the inclusive team would probably be the better option. Many families want their children with Down syndrome to have both kinds of experiences and to reap the different kinds of benefits available from more and less inclusive community activities.

Let's take another example. Perhaps, on Sundays, your brother attends religious services with lots of different people. Later, in the week, he participates in a prayer group that is only composed of people with disabilities. Do you see how the first example is more inclusive than the other? And how there could benefits and disadvantages to both?

One more: Let's say that when your brother graduated from high school, he decided that he would like to work in a workshop setting with other people who have disabilities, packaging items for a local retail store. A few years later, he decides to switch to a new job delivering mail to the various departments at a local hospital. His first job was more like special education, right? And, the second job looked more like inclusion.

In short, the advantages and disadvantages of inclusion and separate special education extend well beyond the classroom walls. The same theory and practice applies to the sports field, religious settings, job sites, and many other environments.

What is IDEA and an IEP?

IDEA is the abbreviation for the Individuals with Disabilities Education Act, a law that ensures that your brother or sister has the right to a public education, just like everyone else. The law was passed by the United States Congress on November 29, 1975, and has since been revised and updated several times, most recently in 2004. IDEA provides instructions to school districts in all 50 states and the District of Columbia on how to educate students with disabilities. As you can imagine, IDEA is complex and has many different parts.

> The IEP is a legal document that includes a specific set of educational goals, tailored to the student's needs,

- **Part C** of IDEA provides for "Early Intervention" for infants and children with disabilities up until the age of 3. Through the Early Intervention program, therapists and teachers regularly visit the child and his family (often at home) to work on the things the child needs help to learn. They may work on sitting and walking, language, or learning skills. All children with Down syndrome are eligible for this program, and research has shown that children who receive therapy when they are younger have a better chance of developing to their full potential.

- **Part B** of IDEA describes the educational services that children with disabilities between the ages of 3 and 21 are eligible to receive from their school systems. A major requirement of IDEA is that school systems must educate people with disabilities in the "least restrictive environment" in which they can achieve their learning goals. This means that schools must first consider educating students in an inclusion setting (as discussed in the previous question). Only if parents and teachers do not feel that an inclusion classroom will meet their children's needs can other educational options be considered.

Under the IDEA, every student with disability is also entitled to an Individualized Educational Program—or IEP. The IEP is a legal document that includes a specific set of educational goals, tailored to the student's needs, which are developed jointly by parents, school teachers, and administrators. The IEP also lists the special services that will be provided to help your sibling meet his or her goals. For instance, your sister might need occupational therapy to help her with her handwriting or keyboarding, speech therapy to help her speak more clearly and in complete sentences, and instruction from a special education teacher to help her improve her reading skills.

Students with Down syndrome are almost always eligible for an IEP, and each year parents must meet with teachers and other school experts to agree upon the learning goals for the year. You might have heard your parents saying that they need to go to an "IEP meeting." This is an opportunity for your parents to make sure that the individual needs of your brother or sister are met during the upcoming year.

While IDEA has made education a civil right for people with disabilities, many advocates feel that the law does not go far enough in maximizing the abilities of people with disabilities. The two national Down syndrome organizations—the National Down Syndrome Congress (NDSC) and the National Down Syndrome Society (NDSS)—are actively working for improvements in IDEA. If you are interested in learning more or becoming more involved, see Chapter 9 for the organizations' contact information.

Can my brother with Down syndrome graduate from high school?

The short answer is "yes," but the honest answer is a bit more complicated. Graduation is a time to celebrate all of the hard work that you put into high school. The pomp and circumstance, the caps and gowns, are a tradition that most people really enjoy. Graduation is probably a big deal for your brother.

IDEA—the law that we previously discussed—ensures a free public education for your brother up through the age of 21. Now, you know that most people will graduate from high school around the age of 18. If your brother were to graduate with his peers at this age and receive a full high school diploma, he would no longer be eligible for the free services provided under the law. You see, according to IDEA, people with disabilities receive services up to age 21 *or* when they graduate, whichever comes first. So, if your brother does graduate on time, he will sacrifice some free educational services.

Another consideration is what type of diploma your brother will receive at graduation. Did you know that some states have as many as seven different types of diplomas? If your brother does not receive a full high school diploma, he might still be eligible for a "certificate of completion" or a "certificate of attendance."

So, what's the difference? A full high school diploma is the highest form of certification that you can receive. Many colleges and universities require a full diploma. The "certificate of completion" indicates that a student has completed his or her individual requirements, but has not satisfactorily completed all of the tasks required for a full diploma. For many people with Down syndrome, this means that they have successfully met the goals of their IEPs (see previous question), but did not meet the school's academic requirements for graduation. Each state around the country has different high school graduation requirements, and many of them now require that students pass a standardized test to receive a full diploma.

If your brother were to receive a certificate of completion or attendance at age 18, 19, or 20, he would still be eligible to receive the free educational services provided through IDEA (because he did not receive a full diploma). This means that he can continue to take classes or other educational opportunities in high school through the age of 21. Some students with Down syndrome stop

Each school district around the country has its own rules about which students can participate in high school graduation exercises.

attending typical academic classes after they receive their certificates at age 18 and then work on life skills or job-related skills through the school until age 21.

You might be wondering: what about participating in graduation ceremonies? Each school district around the country has its own rules about which students can participate in high school graduation exercises. Some schools only allow students with full diplomas to walk across the stage; others allow students who have achieved a certificate or an equivalent to participate. Many parents want their child with Down syndrome to be part of the graduation ceremony after four years of high school. Then they can be with the students who have been through many years of school with them. As your brother's fourth year in high school approaches, you can talk to your parents about the requirements at your brother's school.

Can my sister go to college?

Some students with Down syndrome can and do attend college, but the question remains: is college the best choice for your sister? After high school, most young adults with Down syndrome try to get jobs in their communities. Others participate in "postsecondary educational programs," which can include classes in any setting after high school, such as taking cooking classes at a local community center or participating in computer classes through the local library. Others, still, will choose to attend college with a formal educational program.

Ideally, your parents, your sister, and her high school teachers will discuss many options before deciding which one is best for your sister. They should consider where your sister can best use her talents, and they should certainly listen to what your sister wants to do! If your parents feel that your sister would benefit from going to college, then your family will need to consider the following:

WHAT ARE THE ENTRANCE REQUIREMENTS?

Some college programs require a full high school diploma for admittance. If your sister is interested in a college program that has such a requirement, your parents will need to work closely with her high school to ensure that she meets all graduation requirements to receive a full diploma. Other college programs simply require a certificate of completion or its equivalent.

WHAT PROGRAMS ARE AVAILABLE?

A directory of colleges and other postsecondary programs that are available for students with disabilities is listed on a web page, maintained by the U.S. Department of Education, called ThinkCollege.net (http://thinkcollege.net). If you visit this site, you will see that there are quite a few programs designed specifically for students with disabilities. Often, these programs do not lead to a traditional college diploma, but might focus instead on independent living skills and job training.

WHAT SUPPORTS ARE AVAILABLE?

Your parents and sister will need to work closely with the college to ensure that she receives the level of support and accommodations that she needs to succeed. Remember from the previous question that IDEA no longer applies to students with Down syndrome after the age of 21 or after they have received a full diploma from high school. However, the Americans with Disabilities Act, another law passed by Congress, ensures that colleges or postsecondary school must make all *physical* accommodations that students with disabilities might need. For example, they need to provide ramps for students who use wheelchairs. Colleges are not required to make any educational or learning accommodations that cost them money, although many schools choose to do so anyway.

Under the Rehabilitation Act (specifically, Section 504), another law passed by Congress, colleges receiving money from the government are expected to make accommodations that don't cost money or change the content of the learning. Such accommodations might include extended time on tests and assignments, letting a student use books on tape, providing written notes of lectures, or arranging for seating in the front row.

Before your sister enrolls in a college, your family will need to ensure that the school is willing to provide the level of support that she might need to succeed.

Will my brother ever stop learning as he gets older?

No. Just like you, your brother with Down syndrome will continue to learn new and exciting things every day. Even when he is no longer in school, he will be gaining new skills on the job or learning new tidbits from family and friends.

Your brother with Down syndrome will continue to learn new and exciting things every day.

Because of this, adults with Down syndrome can and should be involved in lots of activities. Learning never stops!

Do people with Down syndrome make friends? And how can I help my brother make more friends?

Yes, just like you, people with Down syndrome can and do make friends. We all like having friends—friendships are part of being human! During lunchtime in school, do you like to talk with your buddies about the weekend's soccer game? Or, maybe after school, do you and your friends chat about the latest episode of your favorite TV show? On the weekend, maybe you like hanging with your friends, going to the mall, or

Many brothers and sisters have concerns about whether their siblings with Down syndrome have enough friends.

playing sports together. Friends make us laugh, smile, and relax. They give us a sense of belonging and are people we can turn to for advice in times of trouble. People with Down syndrome have those same needs for friends.

Some people with Down syndrome are very social and outgoing. Others are shy and less comfortable starting conversations. Individuals who are more social may find that making friends is very easy, while others may have a harder time.

Most of us start making friends with the help of our parents, right in the neighborhood when we are quite small. When we start school, we make more friends among our classmates and through sports and other activities on the weekends. People with Down syndrome do the same. Because difficulties with speech and social skills might make it harder to make friends, teachers may demonstrate to students with learning challenges how to make friends and have conversations with the other kids in class. Learning social skills is just as important as learning to read!

Many brothers and sisters have concerns about whether their siblings with Down syndrome have enough friends. You might have noticed that people don't call your brother after school like they do you. Perhaps your brother doesn't get invitations to parties. Or, maybe, he just doesn't have the same opportunities to hang with buddies on the weekend. If you share these common concerns, here are some tips on how to think about the situation:

- First, remember that quality matters. Having a lot of friends might not be as important to your brother as having a few quality friends. You can only have so many best friends! If there are a few people in his life that he really enjoys spending time with—and he has enough opportunities to do so—that might be all he wants or needs.

■ You might find that all of your brother's friends have disabilities. This often happens when the individual is educated in classrooms that have only students with disabilities. On weekends he may be on sports teams that only have athletes with disabilities, too. As a result, most of his opportunities to make friends are among others with learning challenges. Likewise, most of your own friends are probably classmates and team members. As long as your brother is happy with his friendships, it's not a problem that they all have disabilities.

■ If you're not sure whether your brother wants or needs more friends, try talking to him about it. Ask him who he thinks his friends are and then ask him if he ever feels lonely or wishes that he had a few more friends. You want to do what is best for your brother and having an honest discussion with him will let you know how much the friend situation is bothering or not bothering him. Your parents might be helpful in figuring this out. You might be surprised to find that he isn't worried at all.

■ If your brother indicates that he is lonely or would like more friends, you might ask him if he has any particular people in mind that he would like to get to know better. Consider sharing with your brother how you make new friends. Remember that it's sometimes difficult to strike up a conversation with someone. You and your parents could help your brother think of some things to talk about with new people. Some family members have even tried to role-play scenarios to help their brothers or sisters feel more comfortable in new situations.

■ Next, have a conversation with your parents. Share your concerns that you brother is feeling lonely and you recognize that making friends is sometimes hard for him. As a family, you can brainstorm some ways that might help develop friendships. Maybe you could have one of your friends over and he could have one of his over. Then the four of you could do an activity together, like bike riding or playing a pick-up game of basketball. Maybe at school, you could invite your brother to sit with you at lunch and hang with you and your buddies. If the thought of this embarrasses you, however, be sure to check out Chapter 5.

■ Sometimes, the biggest barrier to making and keeping friendships is travel or distance. Talking on the phone is nice, but if your brother has speech difficulties or just gets nervous on the phone, friendships could only go so far. If you are able to drive and still live with or near your brother, you might offer to drive him to friends' houses and pick him up afterwards. That might really help your parents out when they are busy working or running errands for the family.

■ Your brother might be out of the habit of doing things with friends. He might be fairly happy sitting at home, watching TV, surfing the Internet, listening to music—doing his own thing. In fact, he might like his solitary routines and resist getting out of the house to do things. What then? Maybe your family needs to scope out some organized activities (art classes, theater productions, sports) for kids with or without disabilities, where your brother could at least have some friendly interactions with other kids his age.

■ If your brother or sister has no friends at school, consider talking to your parents about programs like Best Buddies, where people without disabilities interact with people who have disabilities in after-school activities. For more ideas on this program and other ways that you could advocate for your brother at school, check out Chapter 7.

■ Lastly, know that building friendships is sometimes challenging for everyone. Yes, friends make us laugh, smile, and relax. But, friends can also get on our nerves, make us cry, and cause us heartaches. As your brother develops his own friends, he will likely experience these same feelings. Sharing with him your experiences could go a long way in helping him develop strategies of his own.

SUMMARY POINTS

- Having an intellectual disability does not mean someone is not able to learn. Rather, it means that people with Down syndrome might learn more slowly than other kids their age and need more practice before they really understand the information.
- Many parents teach their children with Down syndrome to communicate with hand gestures before they are able to use speech.
- There is no one "right way" to provide an education for students with Down syndrome. Some options include being included in "regular classrooms," attending separate special education classrooms, being home schooled, or receiving instruction in a combination of settings.
- Your brother or sister with Down syndrome will continue to learn new and exciting things every day.
- Each school district around the country has its own rules about which students can participate in high school graduation exercises. Some students with Down syndrome receive a full diploma, and a growing number are pursuing educational options such as college after high school.

3 BACKSEAT DRIVER :
handling your family issues

Families come in all shapes and sizes. You and your sibling with Down syndrome might be the only children, or you might be one of many sons and daughters. Some families have a single parent; others have any number of mothers, fathers, guardians, or stepparents. Whatever the shape and size of your family, how does having a brother or sister with Down syndrome change things?

Perhaps you feel like the older sibling even though you are younger than your sister with Down syndrome. Or, maybe you even feel like you are a third parent if you are the older sibling. You might try to treat your brother like just any other kid, but maybe you end up giving him an extra turn when playing basketball or you look after him when you are both at school—even if no one asks you to. On the other hand, you might feel you treat your sister fairly but think your parents are way too easy on her.

Relationships in the family are definitely different when a sibling has Down syndrome, so how do you handle these differences in rules and responsibilities? This chapter will address these issues and help you find the answers that are right for you.

Why does it seem like there are two sets of rules in our house—one for me and one for my sister with Down syndrome?

When it comes to chores, do you ever find yourself in situations like these?

- "I have to clean my room, but my brother only has to make his bed. And he's five years older than me!"
- "I have to clear the table and fill the dishwasher every other night. My sister is supposed to do it the other days, but she almost always has an excuse—and my parents let her get away with it."

These are just some of the frustrations with house rules that we have heard from brothers and sisters across the country. Perhaps you have a similar complaint about how fair things are at home. Although you might understand that your sister has different abilities than you do, and can't always be expected to do as much as you do, some situations still might not seem fair. Many brothers and sisters have complained that their siblings with Down syndrome can sometimes get away with anything.

HOUSEHOLD RESPONSIBILITIES

In most families that have more than one child, including families where no one has a disability, younger brothers and sisters tend to get away with more, and older siblings are expected to take on more responsibility. On the other hand, older siblings receive more privileges, too, usually in the form of more freedom and flexibility. These extra privileges can make younger or less capable siblings feel like that's not fair as well. Even when parents think they are working very hard to make things equal, families still tend to assign tasks based on siblings' ages. So, some of the things you are being asked to do might have

> Parents are often surprisingly interested in hearing your point of view.

as much to do with your age as the fact that you have a sister with Down syndrome.

Differing responsibilities, however, might also be matched to ability level. Your parents might actually try to have the same type of chores for each child in the house, but just expect your sister with Down syndrome to do the chores on a simpler level. For example, you might have to carry the dirty laundry into the basement and put it in the washing machine on Mondays, while your sister might just have to bring the clothes to the basement on Tuesdays. As you get older, you might come to understand and accept that these differences might be fair, even though they are not equal.

In some situations, you might be aware that your sister can do more than she lets on, and your parents fall for it every time! The best way to deal with this seeming lack of fairness is to open a discussion with your parents. Pick a time when everything is going well and everyone is generally in a good mood. Point out the problem areas and share with your parents how the situation makes you feel. You might even talk about a solution for the future. Parents are often surprisingly interested in hearing your point of view. Together, you might come up with some helpful ways to make the house rules feel more balanced.

RULES & CONSEQUENCES

When it comes to rules related to discipline, do you ever find yourself saying something like this?

- "When my sister and I fight, I always get blamed, but she's the one who started it!"
- "When I take something from my sister, I have to give it back right away. If she takes something from me, my parents say 'Oh, just let her have it!'"
- "When I get caught doing something, I always have to pay the consequences. When my sister gets caught, she always gets away with it!"

At any given time, there is always some imbalance in the family, with one child appearing to get more of a break than the others do. In your family, you might feel like your sibling with Down syndrome is always getting off easy. And you might feel that, regardless of whether your sister with Down syndrome is the oldest or the youngest, she still always gets more positive attention from your parents.

Well, just like when it comes to your chores, your parents might have a different set of expectations—and consequences—when it comes to your behavior around the house and in public. As you might have heard, being a parent is hard! When parents believe that their children are doing something that is dangerous or inappropriate, they need to come up with consequences that will prevent that same behavior in the future. Parents have all sorts of ways that they choose to discipline and reward their children, but all of these strategies share a common goal: to stop you from doing that action again.

Some people—like your sister with Down syndrome— might need a different set of consequences to prevent them from doing the same thing again. For example, let's suppose that, in a moment of rage, you used a word during dinner that your parents thought was inappropriate. As a consequence, you got your video games taken away for a week (the horror!). Let's suppose your sister with Down syndrome uses that same bad word next week during dinner. This time your parents say that, as a consequence, she cannot watch TV for a day.

Now, wait a minute, your punishment lasted a week; and your sister got off with a day? In this case, your parents might feel that in order to get you to stop using that word, you needed a week's worth of sacrifice. For your sister, they might feel that a day without TV is just enough to make the point to her. Your parents might have chosen a different set of consequences to best match your developmental levels. The best discipline takes into account a person's age and understanding of consequences. In the end, though, the intended action is the same: to get you both to use better dinner-table language. Your parents might just feel that different methods are needed for each of you.

Next time your sister receives a punishment that is not equal to yours, think about whether her discipline meets the same goal. (This might be hard to do in the heat of the moment. We recommend waiting a week or so before you rethink the situation!) If you still feel that the discipline is unfair, have a conversation with your parents. Be calm. Be rational. Emphasize that you know you might have made a mistake, but you want to know why your sister appears to be getting off the hook. Careful, though, your sister might also be having the same conversations with them one day about you!

I am younger than my sister with Down syndrome, but I am expected to do more around the house. That isn't fair!

In most families, older children are expected to do more than the younger children. But when the older person has Down syndrome, the younger members are often given a little more responsibility than they would usually have. If you are that younger brother or sister, you might not be happy with that!

Parents make decisions about what to expect from each of their children. As we discussed in the previous question, they make those decisions based on the ages of their children and what they think each child is able to do. Some children with Down syndrome have many learning and behavior challenges, while others are almost as capable as other children of their age.

Parents try to be fair, but they also need to consider everyone's needs and abilities. They may expect more from you, their younger son or daughter, because they know you are so capable and dependable. Although it might not feel like it, this is actually a compliment!

When you have an older sister with Down syndrome, you might feel like you're missing out. You don't have that older sister who can take care of you and teach you things like your friends' big sisters can. You might not get the extra attention that comes with being the youngest, and you have the responsibility that is supposed to be part of being the oldest!

In a way, along with the added responsibility, you do get some extra benefits and a big vote of confidence from your parents!

When you are feeling frustrated about your situation, keep in mind that as your sister gets older, she will develop more skills and be able to do more. Most likely, your parents will notice this and begin to give her more responsibility. If this doesn't happen, you can always point out to them that it's time for a change!

Another way for your parents to divide chores more fairly is to have you and your sister do them together. If you both work together on tasks, you might feel like you are not the only one who has to do everything! You can also begin to teach your sister how to do these chores so that one day she can perform them on her own.

In a way, though, along with the added responsibility, you do get some extra benefits and a big vote of confidence from your parents! Your parents are probably very proud of you and the wonderful things you do to help out around the house. If you think things are really unfair and that your parents expect too little from your sister, take the advice given in the previous question: make a date with your parents to have a heart-to-heart talk and iron things out.

My older brother feels bad that I read much faster than he does. What should I do?

Like so many brothers and sisters, you care about your brother's feelings! You know he is very aware he is the oldest, and he should be the one to do just about everything better than you do. But, you certainly can't help it that you are a better reader.

One way to handle your brother's feelings might be to remind him of all the things he can do well. If he thinks about some of his own accomplishments, he might be less upset about how well you read. You can also talk about the things that you have a hard time doing, pointing out that everyone has strengths and weaknesses.

You should not, however, slow down your own reading or pretend that you are having a difficult time. Just like your brother, you have special talents, and you should be working hard to be the best that you can be.

For further advice on how you can handle situations where you might outperform your sibling, check out Chapter 6.

When my parents are out, my brother won't listen to me when I try to tell him to do things. I'm younger than he is, but I am the one who needs to watch out for him. What should I do?

Because you are younger then your brother, he thinks he should be in charge. That seems perfectly logical except, of course, your brother does have Down syndrome. Your brother is probably very frustrated because *you* are not listening to *him*. You might both be complaining to your parents because neither one of you will listen to the other!

So how do you cope with this frustrating situation? You and your parents both know that you are probably in a better position to take care of things when they are out. But it is very important to understand your brother's point of view. He probably does not think of himself as being less able than you are just because he has Down syndrome. Your brother might really believe he can handle everything just as well as, and perhaps better than, you can. And to some extent, he might be right! Some individuals with Down syndrome have mastered the rules for safety at home and out in public. Some teens are able to stay home alone for short periods and take care of most of their own needs. They can even look after younger siblings with some guidance.

Your brother does not think of himself as being less able than you are just because he has Down syndrome.

This is a tricky situation because you want your brother to feel good about himself, but you want to be in charge to make the situation as safe as possible. To figure out the best way to deal with this problem, set a time to sit down with your parents to go over the following:

- What can your brother really do on his own? Can he make his own dinner and decide when he should take a shower? Can he pick what he wants to watch on TV and get ready for bed on his own without help? Once you identify what your brother can do, you can let him take care of those things without direction from you. You can "stay off his back" about the little things and only get involved if the issue is something critical.

- What exactly do your parents expect you to do with your brother when they are out? Do they need you to check to make sure he doesn't leave the water running in the tub? Do you have to make his snack for him—and make sure he stays out of the candy? When you are clear about your responsibilities, you can relax about the things that are not as important.

- Once you know what you are expected to do, work with your parents to figure out how you can assist your brother without him feeling like you are "bossing him around." You might be able to come up with a creative and clever way to get him to follow your directions. Maybe you can have a race to get ready for bed or make a healthy snack together to keep him out of the candy. You'll be surprised at the good ideas you can come up with. You and your parents might also use "positive reinforcement," or what you might think of as "bribery." If your brother gets ready for bed on time, you'll make some popcorn. Perhaps if he listens to you all night, you'll take him out for breakfast in the morning (your parents can treat!). Think of these strategies as a way of rewarding cooperation.

■ Your parents may want to pretend to put your brother "in charge" of you. You can play along with following his directions about certain things so he thinks he really is in charge. Or, your parents might make a point of having you both work together to take care of things while they are out. They could give each of you certain responsibilities so it seems fair to your brother and to you, too. As another idea, your parents might want to say that you are in charge of yourself, and your brother is in charge of himself. That might keep you out of each other's way!

■ As a reminder of the rules, your parents can write down all the things that neither you nor your brother can do when they are out. For example, "No opening the door to strangers" and "No playing in the backyard pool when there is no parent at home" might be included on the list. These points can also be illustrated with pictures if your brother cannot read. Then, they can be posted where you both will remember them! If your brother has problems with you being the "boss," you can always remind him that the rules come from your parents by referring to the written list.

■ Your parents can also help you and your brother identify what to do if things get out of hand, like when one of those rules is broken or your brother is hurting himself or someone else. Parents don't want to be called for every little disagreement or problem when they are out, but there are times when you need to get their help. Have your parents make a list of when to call for reinforcements and when to leave them alone!

Whatever plan you and your parents come up with, make sure you set the situation up to be successful. If things go smoothly this time, chances are the plan will work well the next time, too.

Should I treat my sister like any other kid, or should I give her more of a break because she has Down syndrome?

Because she has Down syndrome, your sister is different in some ways from other people her age. She might have difficulty with following directions or understanding more complicated conversations. Consequently, thinking of her as slightly younger than her actual age might be helpful. Instead of measuring her abilities according to her chronological age (how old she actually is according to her birth date), think instead about her developmental age (the age at which she seems to be learning and understanding).

> Instead of measuring your sister's abilities according to her chronological age, think instead about her developmental age.

In contrast to your other siblings or friends of her age, your sister might need to be repeatedly reminded of the rules or chores that need to be done. She might need to be shown how to do something several times before she successfully masters it. Your sister might need extra time to catch onto things. However, you and your parents should expect that she can follow the rules, behave reasonably, and have responsibilities around the house appropriate to her developmental age.

How do you figure out her developmental age? Your parents might be helpful with this. You can have a discussion about how much your sister understands and how you can best help her learn the rules. Your sister is certainly more like any other person than she is different. So treating her like one of the gang, who is just a bit younger, is often a good approach.

Should I tell my brother he has Down syndrome?

People with Down syndrome should certainly be told they have the condition, but *your parents* should decide when and how to tell your brother. Depending on his age, your brother may already know that he has Down syndrome or at least be aware of his differences to some extent. He may notice that other children in school who don't have disabilities can do more than he can. Your brother might be a bit frustrated when he needs to work harder to finish things in class.

Even before your brother learns the term "Down syndrome," he might notice other people who have it.

Interestingly, even before he learns the term "Down syndrome," your brother might notice other people who have it. He might even have commented, "That boy is just like me!" Your brother might also seem to be more comfortable with others with Down syndrome than people who do not have learning differences. When given a choice, he might even prefer to socialize with the group of people with Down syndrome.

Chances are, even if your family has not used the term "Down syndrome" with your brother, they have at least talked with him about needing extra help to learn. As a result, he might be quite aware that he learns somewhat differently, although he might not feel that this is necessarily a bad thing. While you might worry that your brother will stop trying if he knows things are harder for him, individuals with Down syndrome are usually quite determined and don't think anything stands in their way! Remember also that when your parents tell your brother that he has Down syndrome, this does not mean they are saying that he can't do things. They are just pointing out that he might have to work harder to reach his goals.

There are a few good reasons why your brother should know he has Down syndrome.

- He has probably heard the words before and not understood exactly what they mean.
- He might feel better knowing there is a reason for his learning challenges. Your brother can use the fact that he has Down syndrome as a way to explain why he might not be able to learn to drive or accomplish other milestones. Many young adults feel that having Down syndrome gets in the way of doing things, but it also helps them understand why they have difficulties.
- Pointing out friends who also have Down syndrome might be helpful, too. Your brother might feel better knowing he is part of a larger group of some pretty cool people!
- Your brother might like going to conferences for people with Down syndrome and learning to be a *self-advocate* (someone who speaks for himself and helps make his own plans for the future). He can still do many things, even with his learning differences.

BUT WHAT IF YOUR BROTHER SAYS HE "HATES" HAVING DOWN SYNDROME? WHAT DO YOU SAY THEN?

Usually when a person with Down syndrome expresses this feeling, he has something specific in mind that is causing

> Your brother can still work to accomplish his dreams; he just might need to go about trying to reach them differently.

a problem. Some problems have simpler solutions. For example, your brother might want a date for a school dance, and he feels that no one will go with him because he has Down syndrome. You or your parents can help him figure out who he might ask and who will say "yes." Once he has a date, he might feel less concerned about his disability. Perhaps your brother wants to try out for the school baseball team but can't compete because he knows he doesn't have the skills. You or your parents can point him in another direction, such as managing the team or trying out for the Special Olympics team. Once he has an athletic opportunity, he might not "hate" Down syndrome, as much.

Some people are very aware that having Down syndrome generally limits their opportunities. The solution to this feeling isn't as simple as the dance or baseball dilemma; you can't take Down syndrome away for them! You can agree with your brother that having this disability can be a real pain. But, you can also remind him of how much he likes his other friends with Down syndrome. You can help him think about all the things he can do well, and you can talk about how proud you and your parents are of him.

Of course, you can also point out some of the real advantages. Having Down syndrome might mean that your brother gets to take a bus to school while everyone else has to walk—in the rain, the snow, and the hot weather, too! Your brother (and the rest of your family) might get to go to the front of the line at Disney World or other amusement parks. He might even get donated tickets to local baseball games when the rest of the world has to pay. When your parents explain Down syndrome to your brother, they can point out that he can still work to accomplish his dreams; he just might need to go about trying to reach them differently.

Over time, people who "hate having Down syndrome" generally begin to accept what it means to have the disability and begin to adjust their goals for school, career, and relationships. If your brother remains particularly upset—and you cannot identify a particular source of his feelings—you should definitely talk things over with your parents.

My twin sister has Down syndrome. I feel like she is always trying to compete with me and always wants to do exactly what I do. Help!

Being a twin is different than being just any brother or sister. Twins spend so much of their time together beginning in the womb and continuing after birth. Often, the babies share a crib when they are very tiny. Parents might also keep the twins on the same eating and sleeping schedule to make care easier. They are often dressed in coordinating outfits and are referred to as "the twins" in conversation. Twins are usually very close growing up because they spend so much time together.

When one of the twins has Down syndrome, however, things are a bit different. To begin with, the babies reach milestones such as crawling, talking, and walking at very different times. Before long, "the twins" are not acting the same. The child with Down syndrome begins to seem younger than her sibling, and the other child begins to take on a helping role, like a big sister or brother would.

If a child with Down syndrome is very aware that she is a twin, she will probably keep trying to catch up. No wonder your sister tries to copy what you do! To help with this rather tricky situation, remind your sister that even though you are twins, you are two different people. You each have unique strengths and weaknesses. As in the case of the younger sibling in the previous question, remind her of the things she can do well. You can also talk about the things that are hard for you. And, you can still do some "twin" things together to make her feel better, like having the same favorite flavor of ice cream, wearing the same headband in your hair, and watching your favorite movie together.

As two separate people, you also have different friends and social experiences. This would be the case even if your sister didn't have Down syndrome. You may find that you get invited to parties, and your sister isn't included. On the other hand, your sister probably gets invited to events that you are left out of! If you get more invitations, though, you might feel guilty, and she might feel sad. Such feelings are natural but should not get in the way of you developing your own friendships.

Most likely, in addition to these separate experiences, there are also events that you are both invited to participate in. You get to have some "twin" experiences, but you both are allowed to have separate lives.

If you feel badly that your sister has fewer social opportunities than you do, be sure to share these feelings with your parents. They know your sister's interests and can look for other community-based activities for her. They can also help set up get-togethers with her friends from school. In situations where you feel comfortable, you can try to include your sister with your friends from time to time. For hints on how to make this happen, see Chapter 5.

At certain points in your life, you might feel a bit uncomfortable about the idea of having a twin with Down syndrome. While you might have the same hair color or eye color, being twins does not mean that you have the same learning ability and interests, so you don't need to worry about having everything in common. You are still both separate and unique people, and you should follow the interests that make *you* special.

In my family, there are only two of us, my brother with Down syndrome and me. My friend has an older brother with Down syndrome, too, but she also has four other brothers! How are things different in small and large families?

With only two of you in the family, your brother has only you to go to when he is bored and is looking for something to do. When he has a bad day in school, he just has you to complain to or to yell at. When there are only two of you, you might find you are asked to do a little bit more because your mom has only one other child to look to for an extra pair of hands!

Within a larger family, your friend has a few more options. If her brother comes to her because he is bored and is looking for something to do, your friend can send him down the hall to find another brother. If her brother is looking for someone to complain to, he has a few choices. And, if Mom asks your friend to help her brother with something, she can try to get another sibling to help out instead.

As you can see, with just two children in the family, the pressure to be involved with your brother can be greater. You just don't have the opportunities that your friend has to call in another sibling for help. If you are feeling overwhelmed by the responsibilities that come with being the only sibling, consider talking to your parents. They are probably aware of the extra stress a small family might cause, but your reminder might be helpful.

On the other hand, being a sibling in a smaller family has its advantages. Your parents might be able to spend more time with your brother, giving you the freedom and independence to be with your friends and do things on your own. You can also get more attention (if you want it) from your parents simply because they have fewer children to take care of. In addition, depending on family circumstances, smaller families can be more "mobile." Taking two children to the movies or the beach, for example, is much easier than taking six.

Families come in all different shapes and sizes. Of course, you cannot choose what family you are born into, but you can appreciate all of the joys and frustrations that might come with being a member of a small or large household. Try sharing with your parents some of your observations about the ways your family size makes a difference in your life. They probably have some thoughts of their own that they can share with you.

I'm always asked to help my sister. What about my own time?

Certain responsibilities and expectations come with living in any family that has more than one child. Brothers and sisters are asked to share everything from toys to bedrooms to Mom's or Dad's attention. They are asked to help each other out, protect each other in dangerous situations, work together, and clean up, just to name a few. And, of course, siblings are supposed to be nice to each other!

Helping each other is expected of all family members, especially if you are one of the oldest. But, there might be a time when you feel you are asked to do too much. Let's examine two different possible situations:

1. YOU HAVE ALWAYS BEEN AGREEABLE WHEN ASKED TO HELP YOUR SISTER.

If this is the case, your parents might think that you are fine with helping out. They might have fallen into the habit of expecting you to pitch in for many different situations. Sometimes parents fail to realize just how much they are depending on you!

To solve this problem, you need to speak up. Find a good time to have a conversation with your parents—when everyone is in a good mood, and your sister is in bed or busy with another activity. Explain that you need a break! Try to give clear examples of when you are okay with helping out

Sometimes parents fail to realize just how much they are depending on you.

and when you are not. Perhaps your parents can re-member to *ask* you first rather than just expecting that you will help in every situation. You deserve your own time; so don't feel bad about looking for some time off!

In some situations, parents almost come to depend on you to be your sister's best friend. This might make you feel extra guilty. When you talk with your parents about what you are okay with and what is difficult for you, they can begin to plan ahead for times when you are not available to occupy your sister. They can plan play dates, go to the park, or get your sister involved in helping to make dinner. With your parents' help, you'll find a good balance between the time you spend with and without your sister. Then you'll enjoy your time together so much more. You and your sister will both be happier as a result.

2. YOU DON'T REALLY LIKE HELPING YOUR SISTER; YOU'D RATHER BE WITH YOUR FRIENDS OR DOING YOUR OWN THING.

If this is the case, you might want to think about how much you do with your sister. Next, remind yourself that assisting brothers and sisters is expected in any family. Then, sit down with a piece of paper and draw a line down the middle. On one side of the line, list the kinds of things you wouldn't mind do-ing for your sister. On the other side, write down things you'd rather not be part of. Try to have at least five items on either side of the line. Share your list with your parents. Again, try to pick a time to talk about this when everyone is happy. Is there anything your parents want to add to the list? Discuss each item with them. Then, you and your parents can use your list as a guide for when they can expect you to help.

Your list might change from time to time. As you get older, you might find that you no longer need to use the list. You'll feel better about helping out whenever the mood strikes!

On certain days, you may find that you don't mind being with your sister. But if you've had a bad day or have a lot of homework weighing on your mind, you might feel like you really need your own time. Take advantage of the good days to spend time helping, and then your parents will be more likely to allow you to do your own thing when you need a break.

Sometimes I feel like my parents want me to be perfect to make up for my sister with Down syndrome. This can really stress me out. Help!

Being perfect is impossible! So if you are trying hard to always get good grades, to be a great athlete, and to always do the right thing to make your parents happy, you are setting yourself up for a lot of stress and pressure. You are allowed to have a bad day, get a less than perfect grade, and miss that catch on a fly ball in the outfield. After all, you're only human. Let's look at some of the reasons you might be working so hard to be perfect:

TRYING NOT TO BE ANY BOTHER...

If you are trying to be perfect because you think your parents have enough to worry about with your sister, remember that parents can do more than one thing at a time! Parents can worry about two children or three or four—all in the same day. They can help one child with homework on one day and take another for medical tests the next. They might even be able to do both those things on the very same day! And realistically, they do not expect you to be perfect. They know that you will need to talk or ask for help at one time or another. Parents do not want you to struggle with problems alone, even if they seem distracted or have other things on their minds and forget to ask you about your day. Most of the time, they can still listen.

If other problems are somewhat overwhelming for your parents to handle during a bad week and they can't give you their full attention, they can help you get assistance from another caring adult. When their stress level goes down, they can check in with you to see how things are going.

> Being perfect is impossible! You are allowed to have a bad day, get a less than perfect grade, and miss that catch on a fly ball in the outfield.

Your parents do not expect that raising you will be completely stress-free. They accept that you may cause a little trouble every now and then!

ASSUMING YOU NEED TO "MAKE UP" FOR YOUR SISTER...

While your sister with Down syndrome has certain limitations, she brings other gifts to your parents and your family. Accomplishments are not just measured in grades on a report card, college acceptances, and careers as a doctor or lawyer. As we discussed in Chapter 2, your sister is an important person with her own unique talents. For sure, your parents are proud of your sister for all that she can do. They know she is doing the best she can, too. They shouldn't feel you have to fulfill all of their dreams for her and you combined.

Parents learn to readjust their dreams as they come to love their son or daughter with Down syndrome and understand more about the disability. They are really proud of both of you. If, however, you don't feel this is the case and you think they are putting pressure on you, be sure to discuss this with them. They need to know how you feel!

WANTING TO GIVE 100 PERCENT...

Maybe you feel that you want to make the most of your abilities because you see your sibling struggle to do all the things that come easier for you. Because you probably have the ability to do more than your brother, you may want to do the best you can all the time. You might also want to succeed so your brother can at least participate as your "number one fan."

Trying to do your best is a good thing. If more people tried to work to their full potential, what a great world this would be! That's not always realistic, though. Even when you try your hardest, mistakes can still happen, and the results might sometimes feel disappointing. Once again, being a little bit less than perfect is actually pretty normal. So be sure to give yourself a break and aim for just doing your best *most* of the time!

FEELING PRESSURE FROM YOUR PARENTS...

But what if your parents have actually said they expect you to get all "A's"? Or what if they act very disappointed if you don't win your tennis match? Generally, parents want each of their children to do the best that they can, and they sometimes feel disappointed when they hoped for more.

Sometimes your parents might be disappointed for a very good reason—they know you can do better when you put in the effort. Perhaps they feel that you should have gotten an "A" because they have seen, from past experience, that you are capable of the work. Maybe they noticed that you didn't really study for that social studies test, and that's why you ended up with a "C." If, however, you study and study and generally get "B's," asking for "A"-work might be unreasonable! If this is the case, you might want to discuss the problem with your guidance counselor or a trusted teacher at school. A conference, together with your parents, might help everyone get on the same page.

Likewise, having your tennis coach talk to your parents about how well you played in your match might be helpful.

Whether you win or lose, your coach knows when you put in your best effort.

If you are feeling extra pressure from your parents, let them know how you feel. They may not be aware that their disappointment is having such an effect on you.

Is it tough to be the parent of someone with Down syndrome?

Your mom and dad might make it look easy, but being a parent is one of the hardest jobs on the planet, regardless of whether you have a child with Down syndrome! There are so many things to teach and so much to worry about with kids. Yet, while it may be tough, being a parent is probably one of the most rewarding jobs in the world.

Children with Down syndrome are more like other children than they are different. But there are a few extra things to think about.

When children are born, they don't come with a guidebook. Parents often figure out what to do by watching their own parents or friends. They rely on their experiences growing up with siblings or with babysitting the neighbors' children. They ask for help from grandparents, too. Many parents also find good role models around them for raising children. A few very fortunate moms and dads might have actually taken a course on how to be a parent when they were in high school or college.

When your sister or brother was born with Down syndrome, however, your parents entered new territory. For some parents, their brand new baby may have been the very first person with Down syndrome they had ever met. Others may have remembered someone they knew in school or in the neighborhood, but not someone they knew very well, who had Down syndrome. A few may actually have had a relative with the diagnosis, and a few others might have a good friend with a child with Down syndrome. That would give them a real advantage!

Children with Down syndrome are more like other children than they are different. But, there are a few extra things to think about. Your brother or sister might have medical issues and therapy needs that make the early years of parenting a bit more complicated. (See Chapter 1 for more on this.) Further challenges may come with the school years. Because of your sister's or brother's extra educational needs, registering for school is not as simple as filling out some paperwork. A special plan needs to be made for how to best teach your sister or brother. (See Chapter 2 for more on this.) Finding friends and leisure time activities can take extra work because parents have to do more of the arranging for a child with Down syndrome. And then, there might be some additional issues to consider for the future: Will your brother or sister be able to live independently, have a job, manage money, behave appropriately?

Believe it or not, some parents also worry about whether having a brother or sister with Down syndrome will be difficult for you. They want you to have a happy life without any extra worry and stress. With all the added work a child with Down syndrome can bring, parents have to be careful to balance the needs of everyone in the family and still find time for themselves, too!

So, is it tough to have a child with Down syndrome? The simple answer is "Yes!" The more complicated answer is "Yes, but…." Parents gather necessary information, find support from others who have children with Down syndrome, and become educated about how to be the best parent for all of their other children. It takes extra work and, sometimes, extra worry, but the rewards can be pretty amazing!

My parents are so protective of my brother with Down syndrome. I think they need to let him do more for himself. How can I tell them to back off?

One of the most important things a parent needs to learn is how to "let go" as their sons and daughters grow and become independent. Parents have to give their sons and daughters the opportunity to try things for themselves. Whether we're talking about the baby who is just learning to sit alone, the kindergartener who is trying to ride his bike without training wheels, or the high school student who wants to learn to drive, parents must let their children try things on their own.

But how do parents know when a child is ready for greater independence? To figure this out, they use a bit of trial and error. Parents give children the chance to try something, and then they closely watch what happens. For example, the kindergartener on the bicycle might be balancing better and relying less on the attached training wheels. The mother or father notices this and takes a chance, removing one training wheel at first and then, perhaps, the second, but keeps running alongside the rider! As the child's skills improve, Dad gradually stops running next to the bike. If the child takes off and is repeatedly successful, the parent throws out the training wheels. But, if he is unable to master the task in a reasonable time, the training wheels go back on.

REASONS IT CAN BE HARD FOR PARENTS TO LET GO

With a person with Down syndrome, parents use the same trial and error methods to give greater independence. However, they might need to keep additional considerations like these in mind:

- Your brother might have difficulty following directions, so your parents might be unsure that he really knows what is expected.

- Your brother's speech could make it difficult for him to communicate, so they might worry about his ability to ask for help or information when he needs it.
- Your brother might do what he *wants* to do rather than what he *should* do in social settings.
- Your brother may enjoy attention and extra help, so he may happily allow your parents to make his sandwich, pick out his clothes, and walk him to school. While another child might complain and let parents know they want more independence, your brother might just go with the flow!

In most cases, parents are quite good at figuring out just how much to allow each of their children to do independently. But sometimes, instead of letting go and giving their son or daughter a chance, parents tend to worry and stay more closely involved. You probably understand that your parents are just trying to protect your brother and make sure he is always in a safe situation. However, if you think your parents are having trouble giving your brother greater independence, speak up!

CLEARING THE AIR WITH YOUR PARENTS

Here are some tips on how to start a conversation with your parents about this topic:

- First, clearly state the problem area. *"You make Joe's lunch every day, but I think he can do it himself."*
- Second, give examples that point out why you think your brother can handle more independence. *"When you are out, Joe gets a spoon out of the silverware drawer and scoops peanut butter out of the jar. He spreads it on crackers just like I do. If you show him how to make his own sandwich, I think he'll do just fine."*

- Third, listen to what they think! Why don't they think teaching this skill would be a good idea? Parents often have more information about your sibling's abilities than you do. *"He doesn't know how to handle a knife. We are afraid he'll try to use a knife when no one is around."*
- Finally, after you all have heard both sides of the story, talk about a possible solution that takes into consideration any concerns your parents have. *"Why not just let him use a spoon to spread jelly or peanut butter? You can buy pre-cut dinner rolls instead of bread so he won't have to use the knife at all. Or, you can show him step by step how to handle the knife and make the sandwich. Then, you can watch him do it himself."*

Your parents will then consider whether your idea can work. You might offer to help put the plan into practice and hope for the best!

Because you spend so much time with your brother, your point of view can be very valuable to your parents. You can help identify problems and be part of working out a good solution that will benefit everyone in the family, especially your brother.

SUMMARY POINTS

- Rather than thinking of your sibling's age in years (chronological age), think about his ability level (developmental age). Chores and responsibilities should be equal to his skills, not his age. Keeping this in mind might help you feel less frustrated and less likely to feel that things aren't fair.
- Brothers and sisters are expected to help out in any family, so even if your sibling did not have Down syndrome, you'd still have to share, cooperate, and give each other a hand.
- Being perfect is impossible. So if you are trying extra hard to make up for your brother's or sister's weaknesses or to not be a bother to your parents, give yourself a break! You are allowed to make mistakes, too.
- If your sister is frustrated that she can't do everything that you can do, pointing out some of her big accomplishments can help her feel better.
- There are many good reasons why individuals with Down syndrome should be told that they have Down syndrome. But your parents are the ones who should decide when and how to tell your brother or sister.
- If you feel that your parents are being too easy on your brother or sister, or are having trouble letting go and allowing more independence, plan to sit down with them for a heart-to-heart chat. Don't yell and scream. Just carefully present the facts as you see them and have a conversation to share your feelings.

4 PUTTING ON THE BRAKES :
dealing with frustrating behaviors

Are there things your sibling does that drive you crazy sometimes? Perhaps your brother watches the same movie over and over again. Maybe he needs to have his sandwich always cut in a particular way. Or, your sister might always want to come into your room when you want some privacy. Let's face it: brothers and sisters can sometimes really get on our nerves. If you feel this way, you are not alone!

> Let's face it: brothers and sisters can sometimes really get on our nerves.

Of course, people with Down syndrome are not all alike, and neither are their brothers and sisters. A behavior that is frustrating to one person might not bother another person at all. Your brother or sister with Down syndrome might not do any of the things listed in this chapter, or he or she might do them all at one time or another. This chapter contains tough questions from real brothers and sisters about frustrating behaviors they have experienced with their siblings. We offer some reasons why your brother or sister might be driving you up the wall and give some ideas on how to handle the situation next time. With more facts, perhaps you can be better prepared for the next difficult moment.

Hopefully, we have included the frustrating behavior that you deal with at home. If your particular problem is not listed here, check out the summary for a general way to handle challenging behaviors. The summary can also remind you of some positive steps you can take to manage just about any annoying behavior from your brother or sister.

Why does my brother always have temper tantrums?

All children have temper tantrums at one time or another, and that includes children without Down syndrome. Every person reading this book has probably had a temper tantrum or two! Temper tantrums most often happen when children are between the ages of two and four years old. They are a normal way for young children to express their frustration or their unhappiness with the rules. And when they are tired, children are even more likely to have tantrums!

If you have a preschool-aged brother with Down syndrome, you've probably seen a few tantrums. They probably don't bother you because you know tantrums are normal for very little children. If your brother is older, however, you might be feeling frustrated by this behavior. Temper tantrums can make your sibling seem much younger than he actually is. When that happens, the tantrums can be very embarrassing! Let's take a look at why a school-aged brother with Down syndrome might have tantrums.

IS HE FRUSTRATED?

People with Down syndrome usually have a more difficult time learning to talk than other children. Because they can't get their point across so easily, they often get frustrated. And this frustration can lead to a temper tantrum. Imagine if you could not express yourself quickly when you had something to say. You'd probably get frustrated, too. Try being a detective and see if you can figure out whether your brother was trying to tell you something before the tantrum.

If your brother is taking longer to learn to talk, you might be helping your parents teach your brother some other ways to communicate—for example, using simple signs or pointing. Over time, your brother will learn to replace the tantrum with better communication. Children with Down syndrome who can talk, sign, or use gestures to get their points across might be less likely to have temper tantrums.

IS HE TRYING TO GET HIS WAY?

Adults are likely to pay attention to temper tantrums; so children learn that tantrums can really get results. If your brother gets what he wants because of a tantrum, he is more likely to try it again some other time. Let's say that you and your brother are shopping with your mother in the grocery store. And let's say that after you pass the ice cream section, your brother throws a fit! He wants some mint chocolate chip ice cream. Perhaps, your mom tries to explain that you already have ice cream in the freezer at home. Or maybe, she explains that fruit is a better choice for tonight's dessert. But, your brother does not care; he wants the ice cream and is now making a big scene in the store. Out of desperation, your mom grabs a pint of mint chocolate chip, and your brother is now as happy as can be. You can continue shopping in peace. However, the next time you go to the store and pass the ice cream aisle, guess what strategy your brother might try? If the tantrum worked last time, it should probably work again, right?

Then, there are times when your brother uses a temper tantrum to get what he wants from *you*. For example, say you are in the family room watching T.V., and your brother comes in and immediately throws a tantrum because he wants to watch the Disney Channel right now! If you give in and turn the channel to stop the screaming, you've just helped to teach him that tantrums work. From now on, any time he wants you to change the T.V., he knows that he can just start yelling.

> When any child with or without Down syndrome gets what he wants as a result of a tantrum, he is more likely to try it again next time.

When any child with or without Down syndrome gets what he wants as a result of a tantrum, he is more likely to try it again next time. You might talk to your mom or dad about ways that you could reward your brother when he acts in a more acceptable manner. Perhaps, if he asks in a polite way, you could tell him that you are proud of him. Then, you can change the channel for him or, perhaps, make a deal that you will turn to his show after you watch your program for a few more minutes.

You can also try modeling some good behavior yourself. For example, if your brother is watching the Disney Channel in the family room when you come home from school, you can ask politely if he can change the channel to what you want to watch. If he says "no," you can cheerily say, "That's okay. I'll do my homework now and watch some T.V. later." If you're lucky, your brother just might pick up on this and copy the good behavior next time! Of course, it's always more complicated to handle tantrums out in public even when you have things under control at home. In the end, your parents will need to decide how they will choose to react to temper tantrums in public. And if you're comfortable, you can try to use those same strategies, too.

IS HE FEELING OVERWHELMED?

Sometimes when children cannot handle a situation, they express their frustration with a tantrum. Let's say that your brother is doing his math homework at the kitchen table. In the background, you are playing a video game in the family room. Your sister has just answered the phone in the kitchen—her best friend wants to know if she can come over this weekend. Bingo, your family dog, is barking at the window because he saw a squirrel run across the backyard. Before you know it, your brother is having a tantrum. The situation might have become too overwhelming for him. Maybe he could not concentrate on his math; maybe he was thinking about playing a video game or calling one of his friends. Whatever it was, it was probably too much.

When your brother has tantrums because he is feeling over-whelmed, you might need to play detective again with your parents. What was going on? In the case above, you might realize that when your brother does his homework, he needs to work in another room where it is quieter. Working with your parents to find ways to change the environment can keep the tantrums from happening in the first place.

HOW TO HANDLE TANTRUMS

Whatever the reason for the tantrum, you might be asking: How can I get my brother to stop when he is in the middle of a fit?

- One solution might be distracting your brother from the source of his tantrum. For example, if he is screaming because he can't go outside in the rain, offer to read him a favorite book. Getting him interested in something else can help him get past the difficult moment. This works best when what you are offering instead is just as interesting to your brother as the item or activity he is crying about.
- Another idea is to try to compromise. If your brother is having a tantrum because he wants you to do something with him "right now," you could try working out a deal by saying something like "If you let me finish my homework, then we can play that game."

It's important to know that temper tantrums do not disappear overnight, even if you do everything correctly! Children need to learn other ways to communicate. They also need to see, after a few failed attempts, that the tantrums will not always work. It takes time and patience. And then, you should start to see things change for the better.

Why does my sister copy everything I do?

All children learn by watching others and copying what they do. A baby will learn to clap his hands after seeing others do it. Preschool-aged children copy each other all the time. If you go to a playground, you'll see this happening over and over. When a very little child copies what you do, you might think it was "cute" or even funny. If your older sister copies you and follows you around the house, it might start out being funny. But if you laugh and the behavior continues, it quickly stops being cute!

COPYING YOU AT HOME

If your sister happens to copy you every now and then, she might be imitating you so that she can learn or practice something. Your sister might be rehearsing the right way to play a game, do an art project, or talk to others. If it seems like this is why your sister is copying your every move, think about setting aside some time to show her the right way to do the activity. Because she is looking to you as a model, you might role-play a conversation or do a project together.

> Your sister might just want to play with you, but you're busy doing something else.

If it feels like your sibling is copying you all the time, then that's another matter. Your sister might just want to play with you, but you're busy doing something else. Your sibling has learned that if she copies you, she can really get your attention! Even if you yell or get angry, you probably won't stop the behavior. After all, if you are yelling, she is getting your attention! You can try taking a few minutes to play a game with your sibling. Or, you can make a point of playing with your sister at the same time every couple of days so that she knows she has some time with you. This might be enough to make her happy and get her to stop copying you. If not, it's time to get help from a parent.

Another possibility is that your sister is bored and has nothing else to do. If you think that is what is going on, you or a parent can help her find something better to do.

COPYING YOU AT SCHOOL

If your sister is copying you at school, or imitating the actions of another student, her behavior can turn into a greater problem. Others might laugh, and the attention might make your sister think that it's okay to act that way. But, you want your sister to learn appropriate behavior and know when to stop. When others encourage the behavior, it's harder to end it! Here are some ideas to try:

- Because your sister is probably trying to get the attention of others and feel included, you can speak to your friends about ignoring the behavior. Encourage them to smile and make eye contact with your sister when she is *not* copying you, but pretend they don't notice her when she is.
- You can also talk to your sister about knowing when to stop. Maybe you can work out a secret cue with her in advance. For instance, tell her that when you hold your chin and shake your head gently, it means "Stop copying me!"
- You can try letting her know firmly when the copying behavior is not appropriate. Especially if she is older, try to speak to her privately to keep her from feeling embarrassed.
- If none of these ideas work, maybe a friend can encourage your sister to stop. Sometimes brothers and sisters listen better to someone else they want to impress!

If all of the above explanations are ruled out, maybe your sister is just trying to annoy you! Brothers and sisters do that, you know. And admit it: there are things you probably do that

Any child or adult with or without Down syndrome is allowed to be grumpy at one point or another.

really annoy her. Perhaps, the only way she knows to really irk you is by copying your moves. If that is the case, don't show any frustration. It's going to be hard at first! But, if your sister does not feel that her imitation is successful in driving you crazy, she is eventually going to forgot about it and move on to something else.

When in doubt, share your frustrations with your mother or father.

Does Down syndrome make you grumpy?

Children with Down syndrome are not usually grumpy. But of course, any child or adult with or without Down syndrome is allowed to be grumpy at one point or another. Certainly, we all tend to act grumpy if we don't feel well or if we haven't gotten enough sleep. If your sister is acting grumpy and you've ruled out the possibility that she's tired or sick, she might have something else on her mind:

IS YOUR SISTER FRUSTRATED?

Sometimes, people feel grumpy when they have a hard time doing something. If your sister is having difficulty learning something new, she might feel frustrated or upset. If she is much older than you are, she might especially feel frustrated because you can do things so much more easily than she can. She probably knows she is older and should be able to do those things. (Read more about this in Chapter 4.)

A person might also seem grumpy when she has difficulty talking or being able to say clearly what she wants to say. If it's hard for your sister with Down syndrome to get her point across because of poor speech skills, she might seem like she's in a bad mood; but, really, she is just frustrated. She might become so frustrated that she just quits talking. It's too much of a hassle. So, while she appears to be grumpy, she is, in fact, simply annoyed that she cannot get her point across.

IS SHE ANGRY?

Other times, grumpiness could be a left-over feeling after being mad. Maybe your sister did not get to watch her favorite movie in the morning. Throughout the rest of the day, even if she has moved on to another activity, she might still be feeling some of that anger, which takes the form of grumpiness. Maybe you have experienced it yourself. Has something made you mad enough that you were left in a grumpy mood for the rest of the day? Distracting your sister from the problem might help her move past it. Try not to bring up the cause of the anger, or the grumpy mood might start all over again!

IS SHE SHY?

Sometimes what appears to be grumpiness is actually shyness. A shy person is often quiet and less likely to smile or make eye contact. Some people naturally prefer to spend more time alone. It's just part of their personality. Does your sister get nervous in meeting or playing with new people? If this is the case, you might help her out by introducing her or practicing some role-playing at home so she feels more comfortable in social situations.

IS SHE DEPRESSED?

Teens and adults with Down syndrome can become depressed, just like anyone else, as they get older. Not being able to be as independent as most other people, however, might make them more likely to feel depressed. Driving, living alone, getting married, and finding a job are just some of the milestones that are harder to reach for adults with Down syndrome. While some of these "grown up" activities are possible, they can take more effort and more time to master. Boredom can lead to depression, too.

If you think your sister might be depressed, talk with your parents. They might want to take your sister to a doctor who can evaluate her and prescribe medication, if necessary, to improve her mood. Your parents might also try some other strategies like helping your sister work on her goals for the future or adding other activities to her schedule so she can keep busy. So, Down syndrome does not "cause" you to be grumpy, but sometimes the source of the grumpiness is challenging to figure out. If you think you know the reason, try sharing your thoughts with your parents. You have a different view than they do, and together you might be able to figure out a strategy to help your brother or sister.

My brother is a perfectionist— everything has to be "just so." Why does he have to be so stubborn?

Some people with Down syndrome might seem like perfectionists because they like to do their favorite activities or regular chores the same way every time. For example, your brother might take a long time to get ready for school in the morning because he combs his hair "just so" and follows the same routine, in the same way, every single day!

Keeping a careful routine is one way for a person who has learning challenges to remember everything that needs to be done.

Keeping a careful routine is one way for a person who has learning challenges to remember everything that needs to be done. Routines actually help the person cope with a world that moves more quickly than he does. A schedule can also be comforting and can help the person feel less anxious, especially at stressful times (like on a busy morning when everyone is rushing to get out of the house). So routines can be very helpful to someone with a learning difference; it's not that they are simply stubborn.

While you can understand why a routine can be helpful to your brother, these careful ways of doing things can get frustrating for other family members, especially when you are late and need to get somewhere quickly! You might think that it's almost impossible for some people with Down syndrome to hurry along or do something a little bit differently.

If a routine needs to be changed because it no longer works well for others in the family, it's best to begin that change one little step at a time. Your parents or a teacher may need to be part of changing a routine that is important to your brother with Down syndrome. If you think something needs to change, talk to your parents about how they can make that happen.

If your brother's routine generally works fine, but something needs to be changed every once in a while, give him a lot of notice to help prepare him. For example, when you know a few weeks in advance that baseball practice will be cancelled on a certain day, you can let your brother know ahead of time and write it into the schedule. An unexpected change in a routine can be harder to deal with. For example, your brother knows he has baseball practice every Tuesday after school. Practice gets cancelled, though, when it rains, and it's pretty hard to plan days in advance for weather! Checking the weather the night before and warning him of the possibility of rain might help somewhat. But be prepared for a little grumpy behavior!

My sister sometimes gets really stubborn when she is angry or when she really wants something. How can I deal with this?

Being stubborn, like a temper tantrum or grumpiness, can be a sign that your sister is frustrated or is trying to get her own way. Sometimes stubbornness can occur before or take the place

Acting stubborn can be a way to get something special or make sure a routine is followed.

of a temper tantrum. Let's say that you and your family just walked into a movie theater, and the show is about to begin. While walking through the lobby, your sister points out the popcorn stand. "No," you say, "we're going to be late for the movie." Then, your sister doesn't move. You try to pull her along, but she is simply not going anywhere. This can happen, too, if your sister's routine always includes getting popcorn before every movie she sees. She wants that popcorn, and she doesn't care if it makes you late for the movie.

So acting stubborn can be a way to get something special or make sure a routine is followed. When your sister acts like this, she is showing you that she is angry or frustrated. In the movie theater example, your sister knows that you or your parents might give in and get the popcorn if she puts up a fight. For situations like these, try to anticipate how your sister might react. If you know that she always wants popcorn before a movie, be sure to arrive well in advance or bring some popcorn from home (if that's allowed). Distracting your sister from the cause of her anger or frustration is also a great strategy to use when she is acting stubborn.

If you're not sure why your sister is being stubborn, try asking her what the problem is. If she is unable to tell you because her speech or communication skills are limited, stand back and try to examine the situation. What happened just before she folded her arms across her chest and refused to move? If you can figure out what triggered the problem, you can work on the solution! Most likely, yelling at her won't do any good. If you walk away, she just might decide to follow you. Then again, if she's really stubborn, she probably won't react if you do! You might have more luck if you try to distract her, work out a compromise, or ignore the behavior altogether. For more information about these ideas, read the question in this chapter about how to handle tantrums. If your sister is still young, you or your parents can always pick her up and physically move her to get out of the difficult situation. But keep in mind, a tantrum might follow!

Why is my brother obsessed with movies?

Just as doing chores the same way every time can be comforting for a person with Down syndrome (as we've already discussed in this chapter), watching familiar movies or favorite T.V. shows over and over can provide that same relief. When the real world is confusing or stressful, a favorite movie always tells the same story. Your brother knows what will happen; there are no surprises.

When the real world is confusing or stressful, a favorite movie always tells the same story.

Watching movies can also help a child learn how to handle a situation or practice a social skill. You might see your brother acting out a part of a movie as if he is actually in the same situation. This can help him learn and improve his speaking and social skills. However, you don't want him practicing those lines from a movie at your basketball game! Your parents might be able to help your brother learn when and where to practice his favorite scenes. Movies can also give your brother something to talk about with friends. Many people with Down syndrome have friends who like the same movies.

Even though you may not watch the same movie over and over, you may have a favorite T.V. show that you watch every week or every day after school that you don't want to miss. You like seeing the show and finding out what happens each week. You might like to discuss the show the next day with friends; so, it gives you something to talk about. In some ways, it's not so different from your brother's obsession with movies. Your favorite shows or his favorite movies can help each of you relax.

Of course, movies might not be your brother's only obsession! He might be just as focussed on his favorite music, playing the same CD over and over again or insisting on the same song while driving in the car. It's enough to drive you crazy sometimes! One possible solution would be to make your brother a CD with some of his favorite songs that are also songs you like. Then at least you know you'll like the music playing in the car! Another option would be for your brother to get some headphones so that he can listen to his tunes in private.

Speaking of movies, my sister is 18, and she still watches children's movies. Is there any way I can get her to watch things that are more for her age?

People with Down syndrome develop at all different speeds. As you might know, some learn more quickly than others in school. So, while your sister is 18 years old, she might be learning things in school on a much younger level. And, her interests might be the interests of a younger person. Her social skills might also be on a younger level, too. As a result, those children's movies might be just her speed! They certainly are easier for her to understand than more complicated or confusing movies. But, you know that watching younger movies makes her seem immature to others, and that can be embarrassing for you.

Keeping in mind that movies for older teens or young adults might be too confusing or disturbing for her, you can help her become interested in movies that are a little older than the ones she is currently watching. Try picking a more appropriate movie to watch together. Try choosing one that includes things that you know she is interested in (for example, animals or bas-

> While your sister is 18 years old, her interests might be the interests of a younger person.

ketball) or one that stars actors she is familiar with from other movies. While you watch, you can help explain what is going on. You can even plan a regular movie night once a week or so and use that time to try watching a new movie. You might even have some of your friends suggest a movie to her; sometimes, advice from friends sticks better than advice from brothers or sisters! Needless to say, it probably *won't* help to tell your sister that her movies are "babyish." She might just dig in her heels and refuse to watch the movies you suggest. Regardless of your best efforts, though, she probably will go back to her old favorites at least some of the time!

Why won't my sister stop invading my privacy?

Your sister might be especially attracted to your things, or she might just like getting extra attention from you. A sibling who admires you and wants your attention is more likely to follow you and work hard to get your attention. Your sister doesn't think of it as invading your privacy—she just loves to be with you! If she really likes your things, she might also not understand that everything in the house does not belong to her.

Another problem with understanding privacy is that children with Down syndrome have people in their personal space much of the time. This happens because they often need help with toileting and dressing until they are older. This makes it harder to learn about privacy because they often don't have much privacy themselves.

You'll be happy to know that there are ways to teach siblings about personal space! With your parents, you can begin to work on the idea that some things

A sibling who admires you and wants your attention is more likely to follow you and work hard to get your attention.

are special and don't have to be shared. You can talk about this as a family and make some rules that include respecting space. For example, everyone in the house can practice knocking and waiting for an answer before going into someone's bedroom. The door doesn't even have to be shut. It's just respectful to wait before going in. Closed bathroom doors should be respected as well.

If you have your own bedroom, keeping things private will be even easier. You might ask your parents about locking the door to your room when you are out so that your valuables are protected. Placing an extra lock up high and out of reach of younger siblings can work really well. The lock can help your sibling remember that the space is only yours, and she needs permission to go in.

My teenage brother is always parading around the house in his underwear. He sometimes does this in front of my friends! How can I get him to understand the importance of modesty?

To change this behavior, the whole family needs to reinforce privacy rules in the house. In other words, no one in the family should be parading around in their underwear! Family members can all remember to put a robe on before leaving their bedrooms or the bathroom if they are not fully dressed. Closing the bathroom door when you are using it can help, too. Your parents can also help remind your brother to put on shorts or sweatpants if he wants to watch T.V. in more comfortable clothes. Using these privacy practices every day will help your brother change his behavior.

When your brother goes back in his room when he is told to put on more clothes or when he remembers to stay dressed in front of others all by himself, be sure to give him praise and at-

If your brother can remember the privacy rules at home, he will most likely remember to practice those same rules when staying over at a friend's house or when he is in school.

tention. Positive reinforcement will help him remember to do things the right way. On the other hand, keep in mind that if you or your friends laugh or make sarcastic comments—like "Nice underwear!"—your brother might think you approve of his actions. Your remark then encourages him to keep doing exactly the wrong thing. If your brother can remember the privacy rules at home, he will most likely remember to practice those same rules when staying over at a friend's house or when he is in school.

Sometimes I feel as though my brother pretends he doesn't understand in order to get out of doing things he doesn't want to do. How can I tell if he really doesn't understand or if he's trying to pull a fast one?

This is a tough question to answer without really knowing your brother. The best way for you to figure this out is by taking a closer look at how much your brother understands in a variety of situations. Does he only have a problem when *you* are trying to get him to do something, but not when he is with your parents? Does he seem to understand when there is something fun involved, but not when it's time to do chores? Your parents can probably help you figure this out.

How much a child understands often depends on how he is told what to do. Some children with Down syndrome or other disabilities can follow simple directions, but not more complicated ones. For example, the direction, "Pass the ball to me and then go stand under the basket" is a two-step direction. Your brother would need to remember to do two things in a certain order. This is harder to understand than just one of those things alone.

A child with Down syndrome will have a greater chance of success if you break multi-step directions apart. First, try saying instead, "Pass the ball to me." When your brother throws you the ball, give the second direction, "Now, go stand under the basket." This two-step direction probably seems easy to you, and you may think it's ridiculous to have to break it apart. But the truth is: it really can help.

> A child with Down syndrome will have a greater chance of success if you break multi-step directions apart.

On the other hand, if your brother is quick to understand when it's something he wants to do, but he seems to be confused when it's time to do chores, you may be looking at a very clever child! In this case, try giving your brother extra attention and praise for listening when he doesn't really want to. This might help him be more interested in cooperating. Praise can work wonders for getting good things to happen. You or your parents can also try turning the chores into a race or game. For example, you can race to make your beds or try to be the first to clean your rooms. The extra attention and added fun can lead to greater cooperation. If that doesn't do the trick, and you still believe that your brother is faking it, talk to your parents. Together, you can come up with a creative solution.

SUMMARY POINTS

- Remember that all brothers and sisters annoy each other at one time or another. Brothers and sisters without Down syndrome are really good at getting on your nerves, too!

- If your sibling is annoying you, try going in another room so you don't have to watch or listen to the frustrating behavior. If you're in the car and can't get away, try putting on headphones and listening to music.

- Another option is to ask your sibling nicely to stop. You may find it more helpful to tell him what you want him to do rather than what you don't want him to do. For example, instead of saying, "Stop playing that song over and over!" try saying something like "Please play the next song for me." Alternatively, try taking a deep breath. Then, think a minute about why the behavior is happening. Put on your detective cap: Is your brother or sister frustrated? Trying to get your attention? Is he or she overwhelmed? Bored? If you can figure out why the behavior is happening, you'll be able to come up with the best solution for handling it.

- You can also try to distract your brother or sister by giving him or her something else to do to stop the annoying activity.

- Equally important, try giving your sibling attention when he is behaving properly, and ignoring him when he is being annoying. Praise and attention can help your brother or sister remember to act in more acceptable ways.

- When in doubt, call in the reinforcements! Ask a parent to help you figure out how best to deal with the situation.

5 TRAFFIC JAMS :
managing uncomfortable situation

There may be times when people stare, strangers tease, and friends don't want to include your brother or sister with Down syndrome. Do you feel uncomfortable standing up for your sister when someone is teasing? Are you frustrated when your brother talks about doing something you are sure will never happen—like getting married? These are just some of the difficult moments you might experience when you have a brother or sister with Down syndrome, and they are very different from what your friends might be experiencing with their siblings.

You can't always avoid difficult situations. So how do you cope when they happen? Included in this chapter are some of the most common problems experienced by brothers and sisters who have a sibling with Down syndrome. Perhaps you'll find that some of your difficult moments have been included in this chapter. Read on to find some real solutions that can help you when you really need it.

Why do people stare at my sister in public?

We all notice differences in others out in public. We tend to look at people dressed in unusual clothing. We sometimes cannot help but stare at the little child having a huge tantrum in the middle of the shopping mall. And, we are often aware of people with disabilities, including those with Down syndrome.

So, it's not unusual that people notice your sister. When people stare at her in public, they may be noticing that her eyes look a bit different, but they're not quite sure why. Perhaps, they're trying to figure out whether she has Down syndrome or not. Or, people might be noticing that her speech sounds a bit different or that she's bigger than most children who are still in strollers. Maybe your sister is the child having the meltdown in the mall!

> Before you assume that people who stare at your sister are being mean or downright rude, remember that not everyone is staring because they are thinking negatively about her differences.

As the brother or sister of someone with Down syndrome, you might find that you are very aware of people looking at your sibling. You might notice every little glance in her direction and, especially, any teasing or laughter. Some people stare very obviously with their mouths hanging open, seeming to follow almost every move your sister makes. These are probably the people who bother you the most! Other people might just glance quickly in her direction. You might even see little children pointing toward your sister while talking to one of their parents.

DON'T ALWAYS ASSUME THE WORST!

Before you assume that people who stare at your sister are being mean or downright rude, remember that not everyone is staring because they are thinking negatively about her differences. Some people might be looking at your sister because they have a brother, sister, child, grandchild, friend, or relative with Down syndrome. They might be a teacher or a Special Olympics volunteer who works with children and adults with Down syndrome. Maybe, they're even trying to figure out if they know her.

WHAT CAN YOU DO WHEN PEOPLE STARE?

Brothers and sisters from around the country have told us that they have tried the following strategies:

- "I stare right back."
- "I stand between my sister and the person who is staring to protect her."
- "I move away from my brother so people don't think I'm with him."
- "I try to ignore the person who is staring."
- "I say loudly so the person will hear, 'People are so rude when they stare.'"
- "I ask the person: 'What are you staring at? Haven't you ever seen anyone with Down syndrome before?'"
- "If it's a young child who is staring at a playground, I try to explain a little about Down syndrome and show the child how to play with her."
- "I wave back at them."

All of these strategies can be useful at one time or another. There is no one right way to react, though some of the ideas listed are probably better than others. Let's say it's September, and you've been in high school for all of three weeks. Some of your new classmates are walking near you in the mall, just as your sister starts to have a tantrum. Your sister is usually well behaved, so you can't believe her bad timing! You sneak away from your mother and sister. You pretend to be looking in a store window and ignore the commotion behind you. You casually wave to the group, and then, when they're long gone, you make your way back to your family. While it may not be the best strategy, your quick thinking got you out of that embarrassing moment. Next time, though, if your sister is behaving well, you might decide you'll introduce her to your new classmates.

When it's strangers staring at your sister, you probably feel more comfortable being protective, standing between her and the person staring or waving back at the offenders. Sometimes, you may even help manage her behavior at difficult moments by distracting her or giving her a hug—and you don't care what those strangers think!

You might find it helpful to think about yourself and your own awareness of differences. How do you usually react? Can you think of a time when you noticed something unusual about another person and felt uncomfortable—perhaps someone with a missing limb or someone using a wheelchair? You might have stared a little bit or wanted to move away from the individual, at first. Taking a second look or getting further information might have helped you feel more comfortable.

Remembering your own actions will hopefully help you better understand why others stare at your sister and can help you decide what you might do about it.

Why do "regular people" make fun of people with Down syndrome?

To answer this question, let's take a look at why people make fun of others at all. Unfortunately, people very commonly tease others who are in any way different, whether they wear glasses, dress "out of fashion," act too smart, appear clumsy, and so on. Many popular movies and video games also make this behavior seem normal and maybe even desirable.

In reality, most people tease because, in some way, it makes them feel better about themselves. They might have their own in-

When people get the facts about something that seems different, they become less fearful and are less likely to make fun of that difference.

securities; so when they put someone else down, they feel bigger and better than the person they have taunted. Teasing can help them feel part of a group they consider "cool." It can provide a sense of belonging. Even if they feel a little bit bad for the person that they are making fun of, they'll repeat their actions if others laugh with them or they get support from people they want to impress.

People also make fun of others when they are a little uncomfortable with the differences they see. This is particularly true with disabilities, including Down syndrome. Most students and many adults have little experience with people who have Down syndrome, visual impairments, cerebral palsy, seizures, and other differences. In order to feel more comfortable with something that is unusual to them, they might tease. This strategy doesn't really make much sense to those of us who are familiar with people who have Down syndrome. But, we can help by educating others when we have a chance. When people get the facts about something that seems different, they become less fearful and are less likely to make fun of that difference.

Rarely, people tease because they are just cruel. Unfortunately, not everyone in this world appreciates the differences in others. If you feel that someone is being cruel to your brother or sister, let your parents or another adult know at once.

The same small group of kids at school repeatedly teases my brother. How can I help my brother?

It's one thing if your brother is teased only occasionally. It's quite another problem when this happens on a regular basis. You might have tried staring, commenting, or even yelling back at the kids, but the teasing continues to happen anyway. It's pretty hard to take on a difficult group by yourself. Here is one approach that might help.

1. *Figure out when and where the problem is happening.* Can the situation be avoided? Can your brother sit at a different lunch table, or can he walk to class a different way so he won't run into the offenders? Can you find some other friends who will walk with your brother to protect him? Sometimes the problem can be handled by changing the scene.

2. *Try to determine if your brother is doing something to encourage the teasing.* Did he start the problem by saying something that wasn't appropriate? Or is he reacting in a way that is amusing to his tormentors, which eggs them on? If this is the case, you can work with your brother to change his behavior. For example, if he ignores them, they may stop teasing.

3. *If the situation can't be avoided, or if your brother does not want to ignore the teasing, it's probably time to call in adult help.* You or your brother could speak to a teacher about the problem. The teacher can deal with the students involved and make changes in their behavior. You can always let your parents know, and hope that they will handle it smoothly. They can contact the principal or the teacher and work with that person to develop a plan. No one deserves to be teased, including your brother. Bringing the situation to the attention of adults would be a very mature and responsible step you could take as a sibling.

Bringing the situation to the attention of adults would be a very mature and responsible step you could take as a sibling.

When other people are laughing at my brother or someone else with a disability, I am embarrassed to say something, and then I feel bad that I didn't. Am I the only one who feels like this and is afraid to speak up?

You are certainly not the only sibling who has remained quiet in this kind of situation. And, you are not the only one who then feels bad. Speaking up in a crowd takes tremendous courage and strength. You might fear that if you do, the crowd will make fun of you, too!

Maybe you have been able to speak up at one time and then felt ashamed to do so at another time. How you respond depends on your comfort level and the setting. For example, it might be easier to say something when you are among a small group of friends but harder when you are in a large group of older teens or strangers. You might feel guilty, sad, or disloyal when you don't speak up, but you are human and that means that you're not always perfect. It **does not** mean that you are a bad brother or sister or that you don't love or care about your sibling.

If you do choose to speak up in a crowd, you don't have to yell and scream. You can quietly state some facts:

- "He can't help it that his speech is slow. He was just born that way."
- "He might have Down syndrome, but he can still hear what you are saying."
- "He doesn't make fun of you just because you are so rude!"

When you do say something, having some friends around for support is often helpful. It's even better if your friends speak up for your brother, at times. Scared to even think about doing this? Some brothers and sisters find it helpful to stand in front of a mirror at home and practice some quick answers. Then, when you find yourself in the situation, you just might decide to try one of your lines.

> You might feel guilty, sad, or disloyal when you don't speak up, but you are human and that means that you're not always perfect.

How do you deal with people who use the word "retard"?

In many middle schools and high schools throughout the country, it's quite common to hear students use the word "retard." The word is often used as a substitute for "stupid" or "dumb" in everyday conversation. Adults even use the word, often in relation to themselves, when they have forgotten something or have had a problem. Even some popular song lyrics include the word.

The "r" word, as we will call it from now on, is not always used for the purpose of insulting someone with a disability. In fact, some people don't even think about the negative connection between the word and people with disabilities. However, because you are close to a person with Down syndrome, chances are you are offended by the use of the word. We have heard this over and over again from many brothers and sisters. So, if it bothers you, you have lots of company!

Some brothers and sisters have even heard others using the terms "Down syndrome" and "autistic" as a substitute for the "r" word. For example, one brother caught a conversation at school where a classmate said, "Do you have Down syndrome or something?" And, on the sidelines of a soccer game, a sister heard a teammate say, "That's so autistic." If the "r" word gets you angry, using "Down syndrome" probably really gets your blood boiling because the negative connection to disabilities is very clear here.

WHAT CAN YOU DO ABOUT IT?

The most successful way brothers and sisters have dealt with the "r" word is by sharing how the word makes them feel. You might be thinking, "The word makes me so angry, I just want to scream at the person!" But the most effective and long-lasting strategy is to calmly share your feelings.

Imagine the following: You are at the water fountain with your teammates during the halftime of your basketball game. Someone makes a joke, and a teammate says, "That's so r_____." After the game is over, you go up to your buddy and tell him what a great game that was. You then tell him that you wanted to let him know that earlier, during halftime, one of the words that he used really had an effect on you. You know he probably didn't use the word intentionally, but you just wanted to point out that the word really hurt you because you have a brother with Down syndrome. Unless the person is just downright cruel or insensitive, you can better believe that he will think twice about saying the word again!

> The most successful way brothers and sisters have dealt with the "r" word is by sharing how the word makes them feel.

Telling your closest friends that the "r" word is uncomfortable for you and your family makes them more sensitive to their use of the word. As your closest friends begin to eliminate the word from their own vocabularies, you might find that they start correcting others. Before you know it, the people closest to you will use the word less and less. When an occasional student uses it to your face to annoy you, your friends might even jump in and stick up for you so you don't have to do all the work.

Depending on your comfort level, you might try some of these other ideas that brothers and sisters across the country have used:

- Ask one of your teachers if you could give a quick report on Down syndrome. As part of the report, explain how hurtful the "r" word can be.

- Ask your coach if you or he could speak to the team about keeping the word out of the group's vocabulary.
- Write a letter to the editor when the word is used inappropriately in a newspaper or magazine.
- Write an article for your own school newspaper.

While you can't change the whole world, you'll find it feels good to at least change a small part of your school and your neighborhood.

How do I include my brother when I am around my friends?

Because you are asking, we're guessing that you don't mind including your brother at least part of the time. So, you might be posing this question for one of the following reasons:

YOU WANT TO INCLUDE YOUR BROTHER PART OF THE TIME—BUT NOT THE WHOLE TIME—YOU ARE WITH YOUR FRIENDS. YOU WANT SOME PRIVACY, TOO!

In this case, you might be able to explain your plan to your brother. For example, let him know that you want him to play a game of basketball outside in the driveway with your friends. But when you come in the house, you'd like him to find something else to do! If your brother is agreeable, letting him know these guidelines upfront might help. He might be happy to be included for even part of the time. Your parents can help your brother stick to the plan and can intervene if he's not so agreeable. You can even figure out a way to signal your parents ahead of time so you can change activities more smoothly. It's great that you want him to hang out with your friends; just know that it's okay if you don't want your brother to be around all of the time.

If this plan doesn't work well, and your brother just won't be happy unless he's with you and your friends the whole time they are over, talk to your parents. For now, you might need to spend time at one of your friend's houses instead, at least until your brother gets better at handling the situation.

Another idea that has worked for some brothers and sisters is to help your brother make arrangements to have a friend over on a day when you'll be having friends over, too. Then, after spending some time with you and your friends, your brother and his company can go their own way.

YOU WANT TO INCLUDE YOUR BROTHER, BUT YOUR FRIENDS AREN'T SO HAPPY ABOUT THIS.

First of all, if your friends are coming to your house, they should expect that your brother will be around at least some of the time. If they aren't too comfortable with your brother, try planning to do an activity that's easy for your brother to take part in. That way, your friends will see that he can join in without creating a problem. You can even show your friends how to include him without interfering too much in the activity. For example, if you are playing a game of football, throwing your brother the ball every few plays will make him happy. He doesn't have to be in on every play, and he really won't affect the outcome of the game. If it all goes well, your friends might be more accepting next time around and will feel open to spending more time with him.

> If your friends are coming to your house, they should expect that your brother will be around at least some of the time.

If people can't understand what my sister is trying to say, should I interpret for them?

If you feel comfortable in this role, interpreting for your sister can be very helpful. Sometimes young children will just stare when they can't understand what someone is saying, and they might look uncomfortable. When you tell them what your sister said, you are making it easier for children to play with her and to see that she thinks and plays like they do, too. But, young children aren't the only ones who might have difficulty understanding your sister. Teens and adults can also be uncomfortable and not know how to react when they can't figure out what someone is saying! If you help out, they will feel better, and your sister might feel better, too. Many people with Down syndrome appreciate the help.

The best way to interpret is to repeat what your sister is saying in the form of a question. With this strategy, you appear to be just checking in with what was said rather than taking over for your sister. For example, instead of saying, "My sister said she wants to pet your dog," you can say, "Oh, Megan, you want to pet the dog?" This allows the listener to then jump in and continue the conversation, and your sister won't feel like you are interfering.

If your sister gets angry with you when you interpret for her, then you should probably back off. As her vocabulary and use of words improves, you may find that she can work out the situation all by herself. If the person she's talking to can't figure out what she is saying when she phrases it one way, she might try to get her point across using other words. She can even try to act it out. If your sister has some success

The best way to interpret is to repeat what your sister is saying in the form of a question.

like this, you'll probably begin to feel better about letting her work out her own communication challenges.

What should I do when my brother talks about things that I don't think are going to happen—like driving a car or becoming an actor?

We all have dreams when we are in school. What was your dream when you were younger? Did you think you were going to be a star basketball player in the NBA or a famous inventor? Maybe you were going to be the first astronaut to make it to Mars? Or, perhaps, you wanted to be a game show host? You still have dreams now, of course, but you have probably dropped some earlier ones. For example, maybe you're taking chemistry in high school and hate it; so you've changed your mind about becoming a scientist. We change our dreams as we grow, but we still hold on to the more realistic ones.

Some of your brother's dreams, though, might be just the typical teenage ones, like driving a car, going away to college, and getting married some day. While many teens will accomplish all of those goals one day, this is less likely for people with Down syndrome. Nevertheless, your brother probably just wants to be like everyone else.

IS THE GOAL REASONABLE?

One way to help your brother with his expectations for the future is to talk about all the things that have to happen before he can reach each of those goals. Let's say your brother is almost sixteen, and he wants to learn to drive. You know that you have to be able to do many things before you get behind the wheel of a car and drive off. You have to take and pass a written test. You have to be able to read road signs, use a turn signal, and work the gas and the brake, all while carefully watching the car in front of you, the people walking on the sidewalk, and your speed.

One way to help your brother with his expectations for the future is to talk about all the things that have to happen before he can reach each of those goals.

When you or your parents point out all the pieces, your brother may be able to see how much is involved. For example, when driving, your mom or dad might say: "Did you see that dog run out in the street?" "Did you notice that the light turned red?" "You have to keep your eyes on the road so you can't turn and look at that pretty girl!" Making your brother aware of all the things that are going on when someone is driving may convince him that it's just too hard to learn to drive.

Some students with Down syndrome have studied and passed the written driving test. If they don't, even after repeated tries, the dream usually ends there. If your brother passes the written test and is still focused on learning to drive, your parents can take him to a driving center or a rehabilitation hospital where they can test his driving skills in a virtual driving situation. There, other adults can explain why driving would or would not be possible for your brother based on his test results. The virtual driving experience alone might convince him that driving is just too hard.

Breaking down all the parts of an activity like driving, going away to college, or taking care of a baby can help your brother think more realistically about what he wants. It's better than saying, "You'll never be able to do that!" When he makes his own decision once he has all the information about the activity, he might more easily accept his limitations. That's not unlike the student who discovers he hates chemistry and decides science is not for him!

FIGURING OUT ALTERNATE GOALS

Another way to help your brother get past his dream is to offer an idea that he might think is just as good. Using the driving example, you can tell your brother that if he doesn't learn to drive, you'll be sure to drive him around instead. He might like the idea of driving everywhere with you so much that he'll stop thinking about driving himself! You can also suggest that learning to take the bus would be just as much fun.

As we discussed in Chapter 2, with more community supports, people with Down syndrome can do things they were not able to do in years past. Living independently, getting married, and going to college are realistic goals for some individuals because there are more college programs available for people with disabilities and more community supports to help people learn to live independently. Your parents or local Down syndrome support groups might be able to give you more information on what is available in your area.

Finally, don't forget to remind your brother that he is just as special, just as important, just as "cool," even if he does not do some of the things that most people do—like driving a car, going to college, or getting married. These are important goals for some people, but what matters most is that everyone maximizes his or her own talents. Remind your brother that he is already doing great things in your family, school, and neighborhood just by being himself. Let him know you believe that he will keep on learning and doing more amazing things every day.

My brother is in love with the prettiest cheerleader in our high school. When he says "hi" to her, and she smiles back, he thinks she's his girlfriend. How can I help keep him from getting hurt?

If you are a teenager too, you know how hard the dating scene can be. People without disabilities fall for the cute girls or the handsome guys, but this doesn't mean they'll end up dating

When he's sad or heartbroken later on down the road, you can be a good listener.

them. It's easy to be hurt or disappointed when you are in love—or when you think you are. Still, people without disabilities are often more realistic about who they like and who will like them back. Figuring this out takes practice and experience all throughout high school and college, too.

Teenagers with Down syndrome aren't always as realistic. They know who they like—the prettiest girls and the cutest guys, and they may not be attracted to someone else with Down syndrome or another disability. However, as they get older, they often become more interested in their own peer group and find good friends and dating partners there.

When you see your brother starry-eyed over that cute cheerleader, you certainly can agree that she's cute! But, you can also point out that she has a boyfriend or is going away to college soon and won't be around any more. You can help your brother notice other pretty girls in his classes or in his social group. When he's sad or heartbroken later on down the road, you can be a good listener. You can talk about times you were disappointed. You can point out that you got over it and found someone better—or that you think you will in the future, at least!

If you've tried all of the above strategies, and your brother is still determined to ask the cute cheerleader to go out, you may just have to let it happen. Once he has his mind made up, you can't really stop him. But be ready to be supportive if he comes home disappointed. Remember that many things we learn in life are learned the hard way—with a little bit of pain and sadness mixed in with the good feelings. Your brother has to learn some things that way, too. And he may even learn them better if he goes through those tough experiences.

When I started a new high school after my family moved, I never told anyone about my sister with Down syndrome. Now I don't know how to bring up the conversation. How do I tell people now?

When you are in a new environment and are trying to make friends, your sister with Down syndrome may not be the first thing you want to talk about. It can be hard enough to fit in without having a difference in your family that makes you stand out. There are plenty of other things to talk about with new people, like your interest in drawing, your favorite music, sports you enjoy, and so on.

But the problem is, even though you've kept your sister out of the conversation until now, you probably hadn't planned to hide her forever! So where do you start? You might feel like you'd be taking a big risk to say anything now. Here are some ideas:

START MENTIONING DISABILITIES

You can begin by working the subject of disabilities into your conversations or your classroom discussions. If it's appropriate in a science, health, or history class, do a project or book report on something related to Down syndrome or other learning differences. As we pointed out in the other answers, providing good information can help others be more open and accepting of differences. Watch for your friends' reactions, in particular.

COMMENT ON OTHER PEOPLE WITH DISABILITIES

If you see an individual with Down syndrome or another disability in the mall, make a positive comment or share some information with your friends. For example, if you see a girl with Down syndrome laughing with her friends, try saying something like, "Those girls are really having a good time!" That would ensure that your friends take notice. On the other hand, if you see a child with a disability having a tantrum in the mall, you have a couple of choices. You can ignore the scene and hope your friends don't notice. Or, you might offer a general comment like, "I guess he's having a bad day. I felt just like that yesterday after our math test!"

It can be hard enough to fit in without having a difference in your family that makes you stand out.

Listen for your friends' reactions. If their comments are negative, try offering another matter-of-fact piece of information. If they respond positively, try bringing up differences at another time. If that goes well, too, think about taking the big leap and make a comment about your sister. Your friends will probably be shocked that you hadn't told them sooner. You can be truthful here and share that you weren't sure how people at the new school would react.

VOLUNTEER AT SCHOOL

Another way to go is to join a club or volunteer with an event at school that has to do with disabilities. Some schools have Best Buddies chapters or clubs that volunteer with Special Olympics or do fundraisers for disability groups. If your friends decide to help out, too, that's all the better. And if they don't, you'll meet some new people who might be more accepting of differences. You might even find some other students who also have a brother or sister with a disability. That could open up a whole new world of friends for you.

INVITE YOUR FRIENDS OVER

Still another option is to just invite your friends over to your house. You might or might not tell them about your sister ahead of time. Many teens invite their friends over and adopt a "so what" attitude about their brother or sister having Down syndrome. They want their friends to meet their sibling and see whether they accept her for who she is, rather than describing her disability first.

TALK TO A COUNSELOR

Remember, too, that high schools and middle schools have counseling departments with social workers or counselors who can be good listeners. They might be able to help you problem solve and support your efforts.

GIVE YOUR FRIENDS SOME CREDIT AND DON'T EXPECT THE WORST

Whichever way you choose to go, you probably fear the worst. But if your friends are really your friends, and they care about you, finding out about your sister should not make them like you less. Maybe they'd even be interested in meeting her and learning more about Down syndrome. While this is certainly not an easy situation to untangle, with a little luck, you could be pleasantly surprised with your friends' responses.

SUMMARY POINTS

- You are probably very aware of people staring at your brother or sister. But don't always assume the worst. Sometimes people stare because they notice something different and are curious, or perhaps, because they, too, have someone with a disability in their own family.
- When people make fun of someone with Down syndrome, you can help by educating them about disabilities. You can point out that even though the person may learn more slowly, he or she still has feelings and is doing the best he or she can.
- If you find it difficult to speak up in response to others' teasing, don't be too hard on yourself. You're not being disloyal to your sibling; you just may be uncomfortable in that group situation. Sometimes, it's easier to approach people one-on-one and quietly give some facts about Down syndrome.
- If a group of people repeatedly teases your sibling, you may need to seek help from a parent or teacher to get things to change.
- Even though you feel like you want to explode when you hear someone using the "r" word, you'll have the most success if you calmly state your feelings. Let your friends know how badly the word makes you feel. Your friends will eventually stop using the offensive word, and will probably help you teach others to eliminate the word from their vocabulary.
- When you are with someone who has no idea that you have a sibling with Down syndrome, one way to bring up the topic is to talk about disabilities in general. You can state some facts and check out the person's reaction. Then you might feel better about bringing your sibling into the conversation.

6 DETOUR AHEAD :
sorting out your feelings

If you made a list of all the feelings you've ever felt about your sister or brother with Down syndrome, you'd be amazed at how long the list would be! Some of the feelings you might include are warm and wonderful, while others could be quite the opposite. In fact, your list would probably include the good, the bad, and the ugly. Each one of those feelings is very real and very much part of life with a sibling who has Down syndrome. In fact, many of these feelings are shared by brothers and sisters who do *not* have a sibling with a disability.

This chapter is designed to help you better understand your feelings, especially the more troublesome ones. Based on many conversations with siblings from all over the country, we've highlighted the most common emotions that have been shared with us, and we provide some ideas on how to handle those feelings. As you read through the chapter, we hope you'll see that having all kinds of feelings is quite normal. The emotions can change from moment to moment, and day to day. Some might eventually disappear, while others might always be part of your relationship. Over time, you'll learn to appreciate the good feelings and to deal better with the more difficult ones.

Sometimes my sister embarrasses me. What's the best way to handle this?

Regardless of their age, brothers and sisters can be very embarrassing—whether they have Down syndrome or not! The little brother who misbehaves in church can make you feel like hiding under the pew. The teenage sister who shares one of your embarrassing moments with all her friends can also make you feel like doing a disappearing act. All sibling relationships are almost guaranteed to involve a humiliating moment or two.

When you have a sister with Down syndrome, though, you become much more aware of the reactions of others. Does your sister embarrass you because of her behavior or just because she has a disability? Do you wonder whether people are looking in your direction simply because she is acting up in church or because she is acting up *and* she has Down syndrome? Are people noticing her—and you—because of the combination of her behavior and appearance? Or, is it just the Down syndrome that brings the added attention and feelings of embarrassment?

At times like these, you might be thinking that your life would be so much easier if only your sister didn't have Down syndrome. Most brothers and sisters feel this way at one time or another. You just want to be part of a "normal" family. No one wants to stand out in a crowd because of a difference at home. Being a teenager can be hard enough without the extra attention for something unusual.

When your sister is on her best behavior, you probably feel more comfortable. But you might continue to worry that she could do something to embarrass you at any moment. You'd be happier if people didn't notice her or the fact that she has Down syndrome. If she acts up and behaves poorly, you probably feel angry and embarrassed, all at the same time.

So how do you cope with these **very normal** feelings of embarrassment? Here are a few ideas:

■ Remember that all brothers and sisters will embarrass you at one time or another; this includes siblings who don't have a disability. Hopefully, knowing that embarrassment is part of being a sibling can help you relax a bit.

■ If your sister's behavior is fine, but you feel embarrassed just because she has Down syndrome, remind yourself that many people do not even notice. As you get older, you'll feel less sensitive about this. You will probably find that you become more comfortable and care less about what others might think about her diagnosis.

■ If your sister's behavior is not appropriate, work with your parents to praise her when she is acting properly. This will help her remember to put her best foot forward when she is out and about, and this strategy might help to keep her attention-getting behavior to a minimum. Typically, the more positive attention you give for good behavior, the more likely she will continue with that positive behavior.

■ Talk to your parents ahead of time about how to handle a possible problem. For example, if your sister will be coming to your basketball game, ask your parents to watch out for possible problems. They can get her to do something else or take her out of the gym if she starts imitating the cheerleaders or cheering for you loudly at the wrong times. Planning ahead can save you some extra stress.

■ Work with your parents to distract your sister from whatever she is doing to embarrass you. You might be able to head off an embarrassing moment by changing the subject or suggesting she do something else. If you are close in age or older than your sister, she probably looks up to you. You can use your influence in this instance to get her to cooperate and go along with your idea.

■ When all else fails, find a way out of an embarrassing moment, even for just a few minutes to give yourself a break. For example, if you are in a restaurant and your sister starts having a meltdown because the food isn't there yet, you can make a quick trip to the restroom until she quiets down. That little bit of a break can help you relax and give your sister a minute to calm down without you standing right next to her in the spotlight. Of course, you can only do this if you are with other family members. Leaving the scene is not an option if you are the only one with your sister! Use this only as a last resort. You want to try other better strategies whenever you possibly can, so escaping the scene doesn't get to be a habit.

■ When you are among strangers, remind yourself that you will most likely never see any of the people around you again. This may help you worry less about what other people think so you can feel less stressed.

I feel the need to protect my sister. How do I let go?

Whether your sister is a little baby or an older teen, it's not uncommon to feel like you need to protect her. Because you live with her, you are very aware of her strengths and needs. Even if she is very social and quite capable, you might feel she needs that little bit of extra guidance to be safe and successful, regardless of her age.

Brothers and sisters worry about their siblings with Down syndrome and feel the need to protect them for many different reasons. Here are just a few samples of what we have heard:

■ "My sister doesn't talk very well even though she is five. I worry that she will wander away from us in the mall and won't be able to tell someone her name or address."

- "My brother is very trusting. He would go with anyone without thinking that the situation might be dangerous."
- "My sister opens the front door to our house and goes out for a walk without telling anybody."
- "My brother is just learning to walk, and he falls often. I'm afraid he'll really hurt himself."
- "I like to walk my sister to her classroom in the morning so I know she's safely in class. She likes to walk by herself, but I feel better when I go with her."

Most of the time, parents appreciate your interest in protecting your sibling. But it's important to figure out when and where to help out.

Even if you are younger than your sibling with Down syndrome, in many ways, you may act like the older child. You are probably more responsible and more capable, so you just naturally look out for your sister. Even when you are not with her, you may find yourself wondering about how she is doing. That little thought might always be in the back of your mind. Most brothers and sisters take their role as protector quite seriously and continue to feel like this even into adulthood. Letting go isn't easy, and perhaps you can't ever completely stop worrying!

Most of the time, parents appreciate your interest in protecting your sibling. But it's important to figure out when and where to help out. You don't want your sister to rely on you because you are always there to assist her. And you don't want to invade her privacy by constantly checking on her or getting in the middle of her business!

Being too protective can become a problem. So how can you learn to let go and figure out how to help out only when really needed? Let's examine a few situations:

YOUR SISTER NEEDS TO BECOME MORE INDEPENDENT

Perhaps your parents are trying to help your sister become more independent. They want her to practice doing more on her own, but you are always there to help out. Also, your sister gets annoyed because you keep telling her what to do!

You are probably so used to helping your sister do things that you can't stop! But you are getting the message from two sides—your parents and your sister. Your parents can guide you here. If they feel that your sister is capable of greater independence, they must have good reasons. Let them explain their reasons. What are they trying to teach her, and how are they trying to accomplish this step by step?

If you can visualize the steps and understand the reasons, you can switch gears from being too protective to being your sister's number one cheerleader. When she has success with the new skill, whether it's learning to take her first steps, walking to the bus stop by herself, or taking a cab to her first job, you will feel better about letting go. While your parents will be happy to listen to your views, they are the last word in making decisions about how much help and protection your sister needs.

YOU HAVE TOO MANY RESPONSIBILITIES

If this is the case, you are probably taking on too much extra responsibility, and you are feeling stressed. It's hard to keep up with your own social life, after-school events, and your homework and still check in on your sister every chance you get, especially at school.

Think about when and how you protect your sister. Could she be successful if you were not there to help? Remember that you have to let her try even if that means she fails some of the time. Some of the best life lessons come from our mistakes and failures. And your parents, not you, should handle most of the worrying and take on most of the responsibility. Remember that you are not the parent; your sister needs a sibling!

Discuss your stress with your parents. They can help you find a balance between being a concerned sibling and being too responsible. You can also talk with a counselor at school, a trusted teacher, or a relative who can help you problem-solve a good solution to your extra stress.

YOUR PARENTS DEPEND ON YOU TOO MUCH

In this instance, you feel like your parents are depending on you to do way too much with your sister. You want to help, but you don't want to have to be quite this involved.

If so, it's time for a heart-to-heart discussion with your parents. Your parents might think you are comfortable with your responsibilities and are unaware that you are feeling pressured. They will probably be happy to adjust things to ease your stress. For example, let's say you get home before your sister and you usually watch her after school until your mother gets home from work. But you are starting to resent that you can't ever stay for an after-school sports event or club meeting because your parents are depending on you to be home. If you let your parents know that this is becoming a problem, they might be able to rearrange their schedules or find another caregiver occasionally to give you a break.

Parents aren't mind readers. They don't know there is a problem unless you tell them. If you are not comfortable bringing things up with your parents or they can't come up with an alternative solution, you might also talk to a relative, school counselor, or teacher for advice.

I worry about what the future might hold for my brother. What should I do?

It's impossible to predict the future for anyone, including a person with Down syndrome. No one has magical powers to look into the future for all the answers! As we discussed earlier in the book, every person with Down syndrome is different. They each have their own strengths and challenges. If your brother is still young, knowing what he'll be able to do when he is an adult is especially hard. If he already is a teenager, however, you might have a better idea of what may be possible.

Some parents may already have a plan in place for additional training, job opportunities, and future living arrangements. They might even have a formal, written plan called a "Letter of Intent." These plans outline the vision of what they hope will be possible for your brother, based on what they know about his abilities. However, even if your parents don't have a formal, written plan, they have probably done a lot of thinking on the topic. So, the best way to handle your worry is to talk with your parents. They can help to give you a better idea of what to expect and what they are planning for.

> It can be a big relief to remember that your parents are responsible for the worrying and the planning for your brother's future.

It can be a big relief to remember that your parents are responsible for the worrying and the planning for your brother's future. Although you probably agree with most of your parents' ideas, you might have some thoughts of your own that you'd like to share. If your brother is a teenager and you spend a good amount of time with him, you know his interests pretty well. You may also have the advantage of seeing his social skills with classmates and your friends. You might even have a better view of things than your parents.

Do you think your brother can do more as an adult than your parents give him credit for? Or, do you worry that he won't be able to handle certain social settings because of what you have seen in school? Share your thoughts with your parents. After listening to your ideas and your concerns, they may decide your brother needs more training for handling social situations or that they should look for other kinds of job opportunities.

If your brother is still quite young, you can talk with your parents in a more general way about what people with Down syndrome are able to do as adults. If there is a big age spread between the two of you, you will be long out of high school when he is just starting. You won't be there to see how he does and to help him out when needed. This might make you worry, too! Again, share your concerns with your parents. They will be there to handle tough moments and can reassure you that they will be able to find help when it becomes necessary.

You can also talk more with your parents about what your role might be in the future with your brother. Look in Chapter 8 for more on this.

Sometimes I feel guilty that I can do things my brother can't do. Is that normal?

Feeling this way is perfectly normal for all of these reasons:

- Many things probably come easy to you, but you see your brother work so hard to do even the littlest of things.
- Your brother is always trying to copy you. He even says he is going to do everything that you can do some day, even things that you don't think he'll ever be able to do, like hitting homeruns for the school baseball team or driving a car.
- You might feel sorry for him because he has a disability, and you know that he might never have the freedom and the "typical" life that you have.
- Your brother is so proud of everything that you do, and it makes you feel worse!
- You can picture how things would be if he didn't have Down syndrome. Or, you might recognize

the randomness of life and wonder why your brother got Down syndrome and you didn't.

> Your brother might not be able to do the things you can do, but he has his own unique talents, too.

With some or all of these thoughts floating around in your head, it's actually hard not to feel a little bit guilty. But feeling guilty won't change anything. Your brother has Down syndrome, and he always will. No one is to blame that he has Down syndrome, especially you. Besides, you both have your strengths and weaknesses. Your brother might not be able to do the things you can do, but he has his own unique talents, too.

Rather than comparing your brother to you, try looking at him for who he is. Maybe you are proud that he's a better baseball player than his other friends on the Challenger League or Special Olympics team. Or, you might be proud that he is a great student in his classes and even keeps up with the typically developing students in some of them. Perhaps you are pleased that he has learned to use a few sign gestures to communicate, and you know what a big accomplishment this is. Maybe he is really funny, and he knows how to make everyone laugh. If your brother feels good about his successes and talents, trying to be just like you won't be as important to him.

Even if you feel a little bit guilty, don't let that hold you back from doing what you want to do. If you decide not to try out for a sports team or the school play because your brother will feel bad, you're not being fair to yourself. You'd end up feeling resentful and angry, and that wouldn't be good for your relationship with your brother.

Everyone has been given a unique set of talents, and our job is to maximize them. For example, going to college might be the best way for you to realize your own potential, whereas enrolling in a job development course might be the perfect way for your brother to highlight his gifts. Because you are each unique and very different people, it's best not to spend too much time worrying about the things your brother can't do. Celebrate his successes, and yours, instead.

Sometimes, I'm actually glad my brother has Down syndrome because I can't imagine my life any other way. Is that okay?

Whether or not you are happy with your life right now, imagining how things would have been if your brother did not have Down syndrome can be pretty difficult. Sure, you may feel that your life is more complicated because of your sibling. But when you imagine taking away anything related to his disability, you'd probably end up removing a lot of good things too: Your friends might be different and so would many of your family experiences. Your whole personality might change—for example, you might not be as sensitive and patient as you are today. And all those lessons about what really matters in life might have never been realized—or, at least, not as quickly—if your brother didn't have Down syndrome.

You might find that there are a few other benefits to having a brother with Down syndrome. Because your brother has learning challenges, you are viewed as the best student in the family and the best athlete, too. Or, all of your friends and teachers come to you for information when they have a question about disabilities because they think you are the expert. You might like this extra attention, even if you feel a bit guilty about succeeding at your brother's expense. And what about the perks? Maybe your

> When you imagine taking away anything related to your brother's disability, you'd probably end up removing a lot of good things too.

family does not need to wait in lines at amusement parks. Or, your brother might make friends easily, which improves your own social opportunities!

Once you start thinking about all of the things that could have been different, you might find yourself deciding that your life is really okay just the way it is. Being happy that your brother has Down syndrome makes perfect sense, and you don't need to feel bad about it.

When I think of all the things my sister can't do, I feel sorry for her, and I feel sad. How can I handle these feelings?

Again, feeling sorry for your sister at times is perfectly normal. You care about her, and you hate to see her struggle and be limited in what she can do. If she has any serious medical problems or needs surgery, you might feel especially sad.

So how can you move past your sad feelings? The answer is similar to our discussion of guilt in the questions above. Consider these ideas:

■ Instead of thinking about what your sister can't do, focus on all the things she **can** do. Despite her limitations, she is able to do many things. There have been times, no doubt, where she has surprised you with accomplishments you never thought she'd be able to do.

■ Remember that your sister will keep on learning throughout her entire life. While it might take her longer to do so, somewhere down the road she might still master things that she is not doing today.

■ Look at your sister's life through her eyes. She probably doesn't see the limitations that others might see. She most likely has

> Look at your sister's life through her eyes. She probably doesn't see the limitations that others might see.

a positive view and thinks she can do anything she wants to do. Although she might experience some disappointments at times, chances are that your sister thinks she's a rather terrific person!

■ Have a discussion with your parents about their vision of the future for your sister. They might present a more positive picture than you are imagining. They can also help you think about all of her talents and successes.

■ Sometimes it is helpful to talk to other brothers and sisters who have siblings with Down syndrome. They have probably experienced many of the same feelings that you do and could recommend some practical solutions. Consider participating in a brother-and-sister conference. Or, if one is not available in your area, ask your parents about finding another family in your area that has brothers and sisters your age.

I am so proud of my sister. How can I share my feelings with others?

Your sister has a lot to share—her funny jokes, the clarinet piece she has been practicing, her ballet moves—but are people taking notice? You know she works hard to be the best she can be, but you're not sure other people can appreciate her smaller accomplishments. Do you think your friends will think you're weird if you're happy that your sister made a foul shot for the first time ever at her Special Olympics basketball game? Or brag that your sister made you a birthday card all by herself, even though nothing was spelled right?

Most of the time, your friends will sense the excitement in your voice and will be proud with you. As they get to know you and your sister, your friends will understand how important these small milestones can be.

For new friends or people who don't know your sister that well, consider explaining it like this: "When you have Down syndrome, it's really tough to do _____. I'm so proud of her for trying so hard and finally getting it!" If you share the news that way, your friends will see how happy you are and begin to understand that it really is a big deal. The extra benefit of sharing your sister's accomplishments with others is that people are likely to mention it when they see her. Your sister will probably feel flattered with all that extra attention.

> As they get to know you and your sister, your friends will understand how important these small milestones can be.

My sister can make me so angry. Is that okay?

All brothers and sisters get angry with each other from time to time. That's the way it is in any family with more than one child, whether someone has a disability or not. Things can't be peaceful and happy all the time. That just isn't real life!

But your sister isn't just any sister. She's a sister with Down syndrome. You might be thinking that she can't help the fact that she has Down syndrome. So when you get angry at her because she's moving slower, or needs extra help doing things, you feel badly, like you are being extra mean. And then, you start to feel guilty as well.

Brothers and sisters with Down syndrome can be annoying, stubborn, frustrating, and noisy, as we've discussed in other chapters. They can be embarrassing and moody and act younger than their age. The list can go on and on. And when you are too tired, stressed, or upset, your sister can really get on your nerves. So, is it okay that you get angry or frustrated with your sister? It's impossible to avoid feeling this way every now and then. Go ahead and relax. You're not a mean person because you get angry. You're human!

So how should you handle your anger? You need to express your emotion, rather than letting it build up inside. While your first instinct might be to lash out and say hurtful things, there are better ways to express your strong feelings. Using one of these strategies can help you release the anger and feel better again more quickly:

- Stick to the facts. For example, say firmly, "I get angry when you come in my room without my permission!"
- Express yourself by writing an angry letter to your sister or journaling in your diary. In it, you can say anything you want, letting out all of your feelings. Then, keep the letter in your drawer or throw it away. Releasing your emotions this way might help you to feel better, and no one else gets hurt.
- Draw a picture of your sibling and the frustrating situation and then rip it in a million pieces.
- Go for a run or a long walk. Have an imaginary conversation with your sister, letting everything out.
- Play basketball in the driveway or do something else that is physical and constructive at the same time.
- Walk away from the situation until you cool off. When you return, you might be able to express yourself more calmly.
- Listen to music in your room.
- Call, text, e-mail, or chat online with a friend to let off steam.
- Talk to your parents about your anger. If the situation keeps occurring, maybe you can brainstorm solutions together.

- Find a sibling group or a brothers-and-sisters workshop where you can meet with other siblings who understand.

At one moment, I love my brother, and in the next moment, I get so frustrated with him! Is that normal?

Stop and think about this. Is there anyone in your life that you *always* love and never tire of being with? Think about your parents, grandparents, other brothers and sisters, cousins, close friends. Does anyone fit that description? Even your parents can get you so angry that the good feelings disappear for a few minutes or a few hours! When you love someone (or even just like them a lot), you tend to have very strong positive and negative feelings for him or her. It's normal, and it's okay for anyone you care about, including your brother with Down syndrome.

Lately, it seems that everything my brother does annoys me. I don't even want to be around him. I'm afraid I'll always feel like this about him. How can I deal with this?

As relationships go, it is not unusual to have times when everything seems to bother you. You might be feeling especially frustrated if your brother repeatedly does certain things that irritate you or seems to be taking forever to learn something new. Sometimes when negative things keep happening, it's hard

Sometimes when negative things keep happening, it's hard to remember that there are actually some good parts, too!

to remember that there are actually some good parts, too! Of course, siblings don't have to have Down syndrome to get on your nerves. If you feel like you are stuck in a rut of negative feelings toward your brother, try these suggestions:

- Instead of thinking just about all the annoying and difficult things, try to look for your brother's good qualities. Let's say you can't get past your brother's teeth grinding and his sloppy table manners. Stop and remember how he's always willing to share his dessert with you or how he is the first one to notice when you are feeling upset. When you force yourself to look at his good qualities, the bad parts may begin to feel less bothersome.

- Step back and look at what is annoying you. Is it really that bad? Do you have bad habits that annoy your brother, too? If you remember that no one is perfect, things might not seem that bad!

- Let your parents know what is bothering you. Can your brother's problematic behavior be improved upon? Work with your parents to develop an improvement plan.

- If your brother's annoying behavior tends to occur at certain times, can you avoid those situations, at least until you begin to feel less critical of him? A short break from the stress might be helpful in the long run. Then you can start to focus on the positive again.

- While some things may always annoy you about your brother, the ideas presented here should help you feel better about him at least some of the time. But if your feelings don't improve after a couple of months, you might need to find someone to talk to. A counselor or social worker at your school might be a good place to start. Talk to your parents, too. They might be able to locate a sibling program designed for students who have a brother or sister with a disability. There, you'll find others who know how you feel. Within the group, you can talk about your feelings and come up with solutions together.

SUMMARY POINTS

- Having all kinds of feelings toward your sibling with Down syndrome is very normal. You might feel love, happiness, worry, and pride. At the same time, you might also feel angry, frustrated, embarrassed, and annoyed. You're not a bad person if you have negative feelings. You're normal!

- If you find that you always worry and feel the need to protect your sibling, talk to your parents. You can discuss together what your brother can do on his own and when he needs guidance. This might help you worry a bit less, at least some of the time.

- When you feel sorry for your sister, or feel guilty that you can do things she can't, remind yourself of all the wonderful things she is able to do. Your sister is most likely proud of her own accomplishments, and you probably are, too.

- People with Down syndrome continue to learn new skills their whole lives. With your parent's help, your sister will set her own goals for the future. While those goals will be different from yours, they are just as important and meaningful.

- While feeling angry or annoyed with your sibling is perfectly normal, try to express your feelings in appropriate ways. Avoid yelling and name calling. Try to release your feelings by writing them down, calling a friend, going out for a run, or doing something productive. In conversation with your brother or your parents, talk about how you feel without blaming anyone else.

- Even when you love your sister, there might be times when you feel especially embarrassed or annoyed with her. As you get older, the things that bother you now might feel less important and bothersome.

- If you continue to feel angry with your brother or sister much of the time, talk to a counselor at school or your parents. They might be able to find a sibling workshop where you can talk with others who also have a brother or sister with a disability.

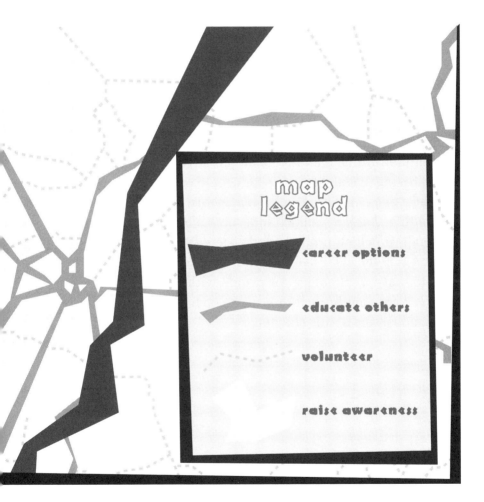

map
legend

career options

educate others

volunteer

raise awareness

7 **READING THE ROADMAP :**
how to become an advocate

During recess, Jennifer, a sixth grader who has a brother with Down syndrome, overhead a girl exclaim, "I'm such a retard!" She walked over to the student and politely told her how the word "retard" made her feel, and then she offered some better word choices. Ahmad, a 14-year-old who has a younger sister with Down syndrome, wrote a letter to his local newspaper, explaining the wonderful things that his sister can do and encouraging everyone in the community to be more accepting of people with differences. Nora, a 30-year-old who has an adult sister with Down syndrome, is an elementary school teacher who has many students with disabilities in her classroom. She makes an effort to help each one of her students learn to the best of their ability.

Jennifer, Ahmad, and Nora are all advocates. Their efforts are improving the quality of life for people with Down syndrome and other disabilities through their words, actions, and examples. In this chapter, we'll explore some of the ways, both large and small, in which brothers and sisters can advocate for their siblings. Whether you feel like you want to do something dramatic to make a difference for people with Down syndrome or you just want your brother or sister to be happy, you'll find several practical tips in this chapter.

What can I do to help people with Down syndrome?

What a thoughtful question! Brothers and sisters across the country are realizing that they can make a difference on behalf of their brothers and sisters with Down syndrome. Do you want the world to realize all of the talents that people with Down syndrome have? Maybe there is an injustice that you want to correct? Perhaps you are looking to become more involved in the lives of people with Down syndrome through volunteer service?

Advocates spread the truth, correct misperceptions, and stand up for something they believe in.

If you are having these thoughts and feelings, it means that you are looking to become an **advocate.** An "advocate" is someone who supports a person or a cause. Advocates spread the truth, correct misperceptions, and stand up for something they believe in. There are countless ways that you can become an advocate for Down syndrome. Here are just a few examples from brothers and sisters around the United States:

- **Educate others in casual conversation.** In your everyday contact with friends, teachers, and others, you can offer additional information when people make inaccurate comments about someone with Down syndrome or another disability. When you casually add some facts to the conversation, you help to educate others without making a big deal about it.

- **Volunteer.** You can also advocate by volunteering for an organization that helps people with Down syndrome and other disabilities. By volunteering you are sending the message to others in the community that you believe people with disabilities should have social and athletic opportunities just like everyone else. A popular organization that many brothers and sisters like to volunteer for is Special Olympics. Visit www.specialolympics.org to check out their activities. Other sports organizations might exist in your local communities and schools.

■ **Start a Best Buddies program at school.** Have you ever noticed students with Down syndrome and other disabilities sitting at their own table during lunch? Maybe you feel that other kids in school rarely spend time with the students who have learning differences. Some brothers and sisters across the country have tried to change this by starting a Best Buddies program at their schools. This program matches each participating student with a disability with a "buddy" in school who doesn't have a disability. The buddies then do fun group activities after school or out in the community such as bowling or attending movies. The purpose of this program is to promote friendship and awareness. You are helping people with disabilities develop more relationships, and you are opening the eyes of your other classmates in school. For information on how to start a Best Buddies program at your school, visit www.bestbuddies.org.

■ **Write an editorial or letter to the editor for your local newspaper.** Is there something that is bugging you about how people treat your brother or sister with Down syndrome? Is there something that you learned from your sibling that you want to share with your community? Consider writing an editorial to your local newspaper. Your voice is powerful, and newspapers love to receive opinion pieces from young people. If you are interested, here's what you should do: Call your local newspaper and ask how you can submit an editorial or letter to the editor. You might also be able to find this information online at the newspaper's website. Find out how many words you are limited to and where to send your submission. Next, write down your thoughts and consider asking a trusted person to give you some feedback. Then send it to the newspaper, as they have instructed, and you might see your article in print! You can also write an article for your school newspaper.

■ **Let reporters hear from you when they report on Down syndrome.** Did a local TV reporter or newspaper journalist write an article about Down syndrome that you agreed with? If so, you can often find their email addresses at the bottom of the articles or on their web pages. Send them a quick email and tell them what you liked about their reporting. Reporters enjoy receiving good comments, and if they hear lots of positive things, they will be more apt to write articles on Down syndrome in the future. If, however, a reporter missed something or you disagree with their piece, let them know, as well. Newspapers sometimes run corrections; but, more importantly, you will be educating reporters so that they are more accurate the next time they report on the topic.

■ **Use People First language and encourage others to do the same.** As we discussed in Chapter 1, people can sometimes knowingly or unknowingly use hurtful words in describing people with Down syndrome. You probably hear people using the "r" word from time to time. Or, you might hear them saying "That Down's girl…" rather than "That girl with Down syndrome…." Model good vocabulary in your speech and writing, and you'll be surprised at how contagious your example will be. And, using the tips found in Chapter 1, help inform others on how they might be able to use better word choices next time.

> Model good vocabulary in your speech and writing, and you'll be surprised at how contagious your example will be.

■ **Write or call your local legislator.** Sometimes there is an issue that needs the help and support of our lawmakers—the
people that have been elected to our state and national of-
fices. Don't let the thought of contacting legislators scare you;
in fact, they like to hear from young people like yourself. You
can find the contact information for your local and national
legislators online or by asking your parents. Write or call your
legislators and share your concerns with them. Some brothers and sisters have written their congressmen about the fact
that their siblings are not being allowed to graduate or about
the need to create more educational opportunities for their
siblings. Sometimes legislators can use their influence to create quick changes. If you are interested, work with your parents to make your voice known to your elected officials.

■ **Hold a fundraiser for Down syndrome.** Many local Down syndrome groups are trying to raise funds for research, educational opportunities, and social inclusion for people with Down
syndrome. You can join their mission by helping to raise money of your own. First, see if there is a local Down syndrome
organization in your area. If there is, contact them and see if
they have any upcoming fundraisers that can use your help. If
not, consider holding a fundraiser of your own to support one
of the national Down syndrome organizations. You could sell
cookies, participate in a Buddy Walk (www.buddywalk.org),
or sponsor a dance-a-thon, just to name a few.

The ideas are endless. Don't be afraid to use your creative
skills in advocating for people with Down syndrome. Just remember that even though you are just one person, you can make
a difference. People will listen. Changes can be made.

Do you have an advocacy idea that you would like to share
with other brothers and sisters? Check out some of the resources, like listservs and web pages, in Chapter 9 to learn ways in
which you can exchange your ideas.

What if I don't want to help people with Down syndrome? Is that okay?

Having a sister or brother with Down syndrome does not necessarily mean that you feel like helping people with disabilities in your spare time! Furthermore, you may have absolutely no interest in having a career that involves working with people with disabilities. You shouldn't feel bad if you think this way. Dealing with the differences in your own life may be enough for you, and that's okay.

> Dealing with the differences in your own life may be enough for you, and that's okay.

Some siblings do develop a special interest in Down syndrome, while others involve themselves with other things important to them—art, music, sports, school government, or fundraising projects for other worthy causes. There are many ways to spend your time outside of school and work, besides getting involved with Down syndrome. You might find that as you get older, your interest in helping people with Down syndrome might begin to change.

Even if you don't choose to become involved in big and dramatic ways, know that you can—and probably already are—making a difference in small, yet important, ways. For example, you can cheer for your brother in Special Olympics events without having to volunteer to help. You can socialize at home with your sister's friends with Down syndrome without being the one to volunteer to chaperone their trip to the movies. You can "high five" or say hello to students with disabilities you see in the hallway at school but skip being a lunch buddy in the cafeteria. All of these are actually ways to be helpful without making a big deal out of it. Do what feels most comfortable for you and know that's good enough!

How do I explain Down syndrome to my friends?

Your friends are probably curious about Down syndrome, and some of them may not know very much about it at all. Meeting your brother or sister and finding out about his or her abilities and personal qualities will help to educate your friends. But, if they still have some questions, you can always share some additional information:

Providing the facts is a great first start in having a conversation with your friends.

- Chapter 1 includes many facts about Down syndrome, including how it occurs and some of the common characteristics. Your friends might have a few other questions that are listed in that chapter. Providing the facts is a great way to start having a conversation with your friends. You can keep your answer short and sweet and change the subject if you don't feel overly comfortable with the discussion. As you get older and have more practice, you might find that you're more relaxed and at ease with any question.

- In addition to giving general facts, you might want to talk about your sibling's abilities and expectations for the future. Describe a few of his or her recent accomplishments or things that make you proud. Once you begin a conversation about Down syndrome with your friends, they will hopefully be more comfortable asking you other questions whenever they want to know more.

If you have **never** brought up the subject of Down syndrome with your friends, and now don't know where to start, take a closer look at the last question in Chapter 5 (page 118) for more ideas on how to start the conversation.

What are some jobs that I can have if I want to help people with Down syndrome?

Many brothers and sisters are interested in exploring careers that involve helping people with Down syndrome and other disabilities.

Just because you are a sibling to someone with Down syndrome, you do not have to dedicate your career to Down syndrome and disabilities.

Sometimes this is because they have seen first-hand how specially trained people work to help their sibling. Or, they begin to look for ways to "give back." They somehow want to share with others the many life lessons that they have learned from their brother or sister with Down syndrome. Some siblings want to dedicate their careers to breaking down the barriers facing people with Down syndrome. Or, some brothers and sisters simply find that a career related to people with Down syndrome is personally satisfying—knowing that you are somehow making the world better for people like your brother or sister.

First, know that just because you are a sibling to someone with Down syndrome, you do not have to dedicate your career to Down syndrome and disabilities. This is not a choice for everyone, and there are ways that you can support people with Down syndrome through volunteer work outside of your regular job. If you *are* interested in seeking a job that helps people with Down syndrome, there are many options. Listed below are just a few examples of the careers that target disability work:

■ **Teacher:** As an educator, you can work in a special education classroom or you can teach students who are included in a "regular" classroom. You can work with lots of students with disabilities and can even advocate for more educational opportunities for people with Down syndrome.

- **Doctor**. You can become a physician who specifically works with children and/or adults who have disabilities. Doctors play a valuable role in advocating for the health and wellness of children with Down syndrome.

- **Nurse**. Many nurses work directly with people with Down syndrome and other disabilities in the hospital or in specialty clinics. Within this career, you can focus on the age and type of medicine that interests you the most.

- **Physical Therapist, Occupational Therapist, Speech-Language Therapists:** All of these medical specialists play an important role in helping people with Down syndrome. In these careers, you can work with children who have disabilities to improve their strength, develop life skills, and communicate more clearly.

- **Disability rights lawyer.** People with Down syndrome have many more opportunities today than ever before because many lawyers have defended their rights. As a disability rights lawyer, you can deal with the injustices that are most important to people with Down syndrome and their families. You can tackle educational problems, employment issues, or medical rights, just to name a few.

- **Scientist.** Perhaps you are interested in unraveling the mysteries of chromosome 21 or developing new therapeutic options for people with Down syndrome. You could become a researcher, working in a laboratory, hospital, or in the community, trying to make advances for the Down syndrome movement.

In addition to these direct paths to working with people with disabilities, there are many other jobs in which you could make a difference. Consider the following examples:

- **Store owner:** Perhaps you want to become a business person, and you are interested in running a big store. Maybe, as the chief executive you might develop a policy that encourages people with Down syndrome to work for your company.

- **Writer or journalist:** There are many stories about people with Down syndrome that have yet to be told. If you become a writer or a journalist, you could share with the world some of your experiences living with your brother or sister who has Down syndrome. Doing so will increase public understanding of issues facing people with Down syndrome. You might even write a novel that includes a character with Down syndrome.

- **Nutritionist or Dietitian:** Maybe you like helping people lead a healthy lifestyle, teaching them to make good food choices. Nutritionists can work with people with Down syndrome and other disabilities, helping to address conditions like celiac disease and obesity that we discussed in Chapter 1.

- **Social Worker:** Social workers are involved in a variety of settings, including hospitals, where they try to make sure that a person is connected with available community resources. For example, a hospital social worker might help a person in the hospital get food stamps or find better housing. Other social workers might help people with disabilities locate recreation or job training programs that might be of benefit. Additionally, some social workers work directly for agencies that assist people with disabilities. Still others may run sibling support groups for brothers and sisters of individuals with disabilities or specialize in counseling people with disabilities to help them deal with depression or other problems.

What might I have to do to help my sister when we're grown up?

The roles of adult siblings vary based on their sibling's needs and their family's requests. If you are asking yourself this question, you might consider having a discussion with your parents. They probably have some thoughts of their own, and having a conversation with them should give you a sense of what they are thinking. You should also let them know what you have in mind!

People with Down syndrome have many different living options today.

Perhaps what you really want to know is if your sister will one day have to live with you. Some brothers and sisters do welcome their siblings into their homes when their parents are unable to do so. However, this is not necessarily the only solution.

People with Down syndrome have many different living options today. Some live on their own or with a roommate and may just need a counselor or family member to stop in occasionally to help them with planning meals, budgeting, and the like. Others live in group home settings with other people who have or do not have disabilities. Staff at the group home may do the cooking and housekeeping or may supervise the residents in doing these tasks. In some cases, staff live in the group home, so they can always be available. In other cases, staff come to the home at times during the day when residents need them most. To determine what might be possible for your sibling, you should have a conversation with your parents and your sister.

Although your sister might not actually live with you when you are both adults, many siblings do take some responsibility for their brother or sister with Down syndrome. Here are a few of the ways you might choose to help your sister in the future:

- Visit your sister and take her shopping or out to dinner.

- Help with money matters, such as helping to pay her bills or balance her checkbook.

> *S*uggest that your parents write down some of their ideas so that their thoughts can serve as a guide for her care in the future.

- Make doctor's appointments for her and follow up to make sure she is taking medications or following her doctor's advice.
- Arrange social opportunities, helping to set up transportation to get her to and from friends' homes, the movies, etc.
- Include her in holiday events and family gatherings.
- Routinely evaluate her living arrangements through your own observations and conversations with your sister. Make any changes, as needed, to keep her safe and happy.
- Help her with any personal or work problems by being a good listener and following up as needed to make sure she is happy and in a good situation.
- Help with meal planning and shopping to ensure that she is eating well and taking good care of herself.

Depending on the age of your brother or sister with Down syndrome, your parents may have already made plans for the future. They may have made some notes about their plans and ideas, or written them down more formally, in something called a "Letter of Intent."

When you are having a conversation with your parents on this topic, you can ask if they have put anything in writing. If not, you can spend some time talking about the future and what they hope will be possible for your sister. Suggest that your parents write down some of their ideas so that their thoughts can serve as a guide for her care in the future. This way, you and your other siblings, if you have any, won't have to make all the decisions when your parents are no longer around. Having a written list of your sister's doctors, social connections, and other important information is helpful, too, and is often included in a "Letter of Intent."

If your parents have not developed a Letter of Intent—or have not heard of one—you can refer them to the book, *The Special Needs Planning Guide*, by John Nadworny and Cynthia Haddad. Parents can also download, for free, a fill-in-the-blanks Letter of Intent assembled by Jo Ann Simons, the mother of a young adult with Down syndrome. The document is called "Footprints for the Future" and can be found under "Resources" at www.theemarc.org.

How can I start a conversation with my parents to ask questions about my brother and Down syndrome?

Most likely, your parents have shared information with you from time to time about your brother with Down syndrome. Additionally, you know quite a bit about your brother—how he learns, what he enjoys, what his strengths and his struggles are. You might even know more about his interests than your parents! But, you may have some questions about things that are not discussed as frequently, like any medical problems he might have, school issues, or your parents' expectations for you and your brother in the future. Having this information will help you be a better advocate for your brother now and in the future.

When you think about talking with your parents about more difficult issues, you might feel a bit reluctant to bring things up. If everyone is happy and having a great day, you might not want to upset your parents by introducing the topic. In most cases, however, parents are happy to clear up your concerns and answer your questions. If you don't ask questions, your parents won't know that you need more information. Believe it or not, parents aren't mind readers. Usually, they don't know what you

If you don't ask questions, your parents won't know that you need more information.

are thinking unless you let them know! As you get older, you might find it easier to talk with your parents about Down syndrome. However, there is no need to wait until that day if you have some pressing questions.

Here are some suggestions on how to start those important conversations with your parents:

- Choose a time when they aren't busy and you know they have some time to talk.
- If possible, make it a time when your sibling isn't around so you won't be talking about your brother in front of him.
- If it's almost impossible to get a minute when your parents have time and your brother isn't around, you might need to make a date with them for a time that is convenient for everyone. Put the date on the calendar so you will all remember to set aside the time.
- Start the conversation by letting your parents know you have some questions. To help them listen to what you are saying, you might want to state what's on your mind and why it's been worrying you.
- If the answers you get aren't detailed enough, ask follow-up questions. Asking for additional input will help you understand the information much better, too.
- If your parents tell you not to worry, that they have it all under control, feel free to ask for clarification. Explain that you have some questions and would feel better if you knew their thoughts.

If I don't feel comfortable talking to my parents about Down syndrome, who else can I turn to?

If, after reading the previous question and answer, you still feel uncomfortable approaching your parents with questions about Down syndrome, think about who else you might be able to talk to. Finding someone to speak with is very important. Asking questions and getting answers helps you handle life a whole lot better! Other people you can approach include:

- A trusted aunt, uncle, or, perhaps, a grandparent
- A teacher or guidance counselor at school
- Your family doctor
- If you have a local sibling support group in your area, the social worker or sibling program coordinator
- An older brother or sister within your own family
- Another brother or sister who has a sibling with Down syndrome

A*sking questions and getting answers helps you handle life a whole lot better!*

While very good general information on Down syndrome can be found in books such as this one, or on recommended websites, talking with someone directly is generally more valuable, especially if the person knows your brother or sister. Think about the possibilities listed here and then focus on who those people are in your life. Pick the person you think would be the best listener and give the best advice. Remember, there is no such thing as a silly question. If you have a question, you need an answer!

SUMMARY POINTS

- An "advocate" is someone who supports a person or cause. You can become an advocate for people with Down syndrome in many ways, both big and small. Volunteering, writing letters to your local newspapers, and modeling sensitive language are just a few of those ways.

- If you are interested in having a job that benefits people with Down syndrome one day, you have many career options such as becoming a doctor, social worker, teacher, or disability rights lawyer.

- Just because you have a brother or sister with Down syndrome does not mean that you have to advocate or choose a career that helps people with disabilities. Dealing with the differences in your own life may be enough for you, and that's okay.

- When explaining Down syndrome to your friends for the first time, start with the facts and then talk about some of the abilities and accomplishments of your brother or sister.

- People with Down syndrome have many living options today. Some brothers and sisters, when they are adults, might welcome their sibling with Down syndrome into their own homes. However, there are also many other opportunities for adults with Down syndrome to live independent lives with appropriate supports.

- If you are thinking about your sibling's future, ask your parents to share some of their plans for your brother and sister. This might take the form of a "Letter of Intent," a document that includes information you would need to know about your sibling when your parents are no longer around.

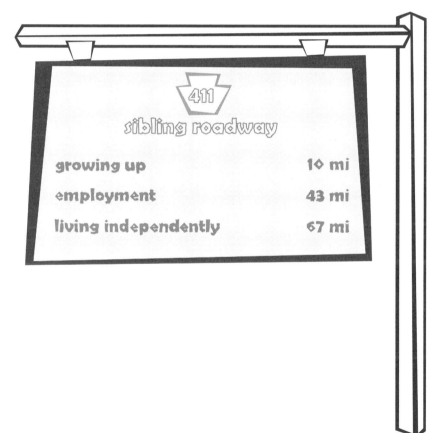

8 "ARE WE THERE YET?": looking toward the future

The idea that your brother or sister will grow up into an adult one day might seem like a distant reality at the moment. However, many brothers and sisters around the country start to ask questions about their sibling's future far before they become full-grown adults. Perhaps, you are concerned about what will happen when your brother gets older: Will he get married? Will he live on his own? Maybe your sister will be graduating from high school and you are wondering where she will work and what types of jobs are even possible.

This chapter takes a look into the future of your brother or sister. Adults with Down syndrome have opportunities today that never before existed, and we want to share with you the possibilities and realities of living with Down syndrome as an adult.

Can people with Down syndrome date?

As people with Down syndrome enter their teen years and beyond, they most likely will experience all of the joys and complications that come with being in love. Your teenage sister with Down syndrome might have a crush on a popular T.V. star and tape magazine pictures of him all over her bedroom. Your brother might begin to notice the pretty girls in high school and want to ask one of them to the homecoming dance. And, who knows, your sister might find a boyfriend and go on frequent dates. In short, all of the emotions that come with love—happiness, bashfulness, compassion, jealousy, to name a few—are shared by people with and without disabilities.

People with Down syndrome, however, might have fewer opportunities to explore love when they get older. If you want to go with a date to the movies, how do you get there if you cannot drive? If you want to see your boyfriend who lives in another town, how do you make that happen on a regular basis? If you want to take someone out to dinner on a date, how will you pay for it if you aren't given opportunities to earn an income? These are just some of the questions that teens and young adults with Down syndrome often confront when they are interested in dating. Unfortunately, transportation and lack of money can prevent them from going on dates as much as they would like to.

If your brother or sister is facing these kinds of obstacles to dating, you and your parents can consider some of the following options:

- Your parents or you (if you can drive) could take your sibling with Down syndrome to his or her date's house. Or, you can arrange to provide the transportation for the couple to go on a date, dropping them off and picking them up at designated times.

- If you are dating someone, maybe you could suggest a double date with your sibling and his or her date. Even if you are not dating, you can offer ideas of things to do with a girlfriend or boyfriend. Try ice cream or miniature golf in the summer. Apple picking or hay rides work well in the fall, and sledding and ice skating are good double date options in the winter, if you live in a snowy climate.

■ If your brother or sister is trying to figure out how to purchase a gift for his date, you might offer some tips on budgeting. Work with your sibling to figure out how he can save some money from his paycheck or savings to work toward buying that special someone a memorable gift.

WHAT IF YOU SIBLING HAS AN UNREASONABLE DATING GOAL?

You hate to break it to your brother, but he is not going to end up dating the lead actress on his favorite T.V. show. And, you know that the star quarterback is probably not going to ask your sister to the prom. What should you do? Remember that having crushes—including seemingly unreachable ones—is a regular part of growing up. Also, remember that heartbreaks and heartaches are unfortunately also part of the equation.

> If your brother or sister has a crush that seems misplaced, you can probably let it be.

If your brother or sister has a crush that seems misplaced, you can probably let it be. Your brother will slowly learn what is realistic and will modify his wishes as he grows up, just like you probably have over time. Usually the worst thing that can happen is that your brother or sister might ask their heartthrob out on a date and be rejected. If you feel your sibling is spending way too much time and energy on an unrealistic dating goal, talk with your parents about how you might help to redirect your sibling's sights.

WHAT IF YOUR SIBLING WOULD LIKE TO DATE, BUT YOUR PARENTS ARE NOT COMFORTABLE WITH ALLOWING THIS TO HAPPEN?

If your parents feel this way, they may have some very good reasons! Your sister may be too young to date even though she might really want to have this experience. Even if she is 16 or 17, a more typical age to begin dating, your parents might feel that she still does not have the maturity to understand what is involved in dating. Your parents may worry that she will not behave appropriately in public and may think she believes that one date means she is getting married!

Sometimes, parents simply find it difficult to believe that their sons and daughters are growing up and developing mature feelings for another person. Moms and dads spend so much time raising their children that they might not notice that things change! Your parents might also feel overprotective of their child who has Down syndrome and might even feel that he or she will never really be an adult. So, if your sibling develops romantic feelings for someone, your parents might be completely surprised. If this is the reason that your parents are uncomfortable with your brother or sister dating, you might remind them that your sibling is growing up just like everyone else.

Even if your parents are comfortable with your sister dating, they are probably very aware that young people with Down syndrome or other disabilities might need more supervision or parental involvement on a date. Allowing a son or daughter to date often means they have to make the arrangements for where and when the date will take place and coordinate who will drive. Your parents may even think the couple needs to be supervised, so they might go along to the movies—but sit a few rows back!

For these reasons, many individuals with Down syndrome begin their dating experience as part of a group. This is how many young people, with or without disabilities, start to date. Maybe a group of young people are going to the movies or bowling. Your brother might want to have your parents drive to pick up his girlfriend and take them both to the bowling alley. At some of these group teen events, there is even prearranged parental supervision or staff supervision. If your parents are resistant to your brother dating—but you know that he is ready to jump into the dating scene—talk with your parents about group opportunities that might be available in your community.

Can my sister with Down syndrome get married one day?

For many people, marriage is an important life milestone, one that is full of many responsibilities and important considerations. For other people, staying single, with or without dating, is the right decision. Today, marriage is certainly a possibility for some people with Down syndrome; whether it is the best option for your sister is a decision that she will need to carefully consider with those she trusts and loves.

There are many people with Down syndrome living in the United States and around the world who have decided that marriage is the right choice for them. So far, no researcher has counted the number of marriages, but the number is still relatively small.

Some of the barriers to dating that we discussed in the previous question become even more limiting when it comes to marriage: Where will the couple live? How will they get around, and will they need some extra assistance when it comes to daily tasks? How will they pay for their food and weekly supplies? Some states actually have programs to assist people with disabilities who would like to become married and live on their own. In other cases, family members and advocates can help find resources within the community to enable people with Down syndrome to live as independently as possible when they are married. Married couples with Down syndrome would probably agree that many people need to be involved to help make their marriage a reality.

> Married couples with Down syndrome would probably agree that many people need to be involved to help make their marriage a reality.

If your sister is old enough to think about her future, she probably imagines that she will get married one day. You might want to have a conversation with your parents to get a sense of their vision of her future. Do they think that marriage is possible? Or do they expect that she will remain single and live with a roommate or a group of friends? As your sister gets older, she will have more to say for herself on this subject! If she wants to get married, there are many things she will need to learn, including cooking, cleaning, and making joint decisions with a partner, to name just a few. If marriage is your sister's goal, she can start working on the skills needed to make her dream possible. Then, she needs to find the right person to marry!

If your sister talks about her future marriage plans with you—whether she is playing house at age 5 or having a serious conversation at age 20—you can be a good listener and help her to think about all the possibilities. Then, your parents can follow up at a later time. Maybe there is someone out there for your sister, but, then again, maybe there is not. Being married certainly isn't the only option. Your sister can be happy as a single adult, as well.

Can people with Down syndrome have children?

Both men and women with Down syndrome have lower fertility rates than most people, with men more affected than women. If someone with Down syndrome does have a baby with someone who does *not* have Down syndrome, the chances that

If your sister or brother is interested in having children, they should discuss their feelings with people they trust and love.

the baby will have Down syndrome can be as high as 50 percent. If two people with Down syndrome were to have a baby together, the chances that their baby will have Down syndrome would increase to about 67 percent. However, as far as we know, no couple with Down syndrome has yet had a baby together. Additionally, pregnant women with Down syndrome are more likely to have a miscarriage or give birth to a tiny, premature baby. With all this said, there are a few documented cases of adults with Down syndrome giving birth to babies who do not have Down syndrome and are otherwise healthy.

The decision to have children involves serious and important considerations. If your sister or brother is interested in having children, they should discuss their feelings with people they trust and love. Raising a child is a tremendous amount of work. Caring for an infant is not just a matter of changing diapers and making bottles. Parents also have to figure out what the crying baby wants: Does he need to burp? Is he bored? Is he hungry? Parents have to wake up in the middle of the night when their baby cries and take him to the doctor when he is sick. Parents also have to watch out for dangerous situations and "child proof" the home so their baby won't get hurt. Some of these decisions are quite difficult for people with Down syndrome to make on their own.

Because so much is involved in raising a child, most people with Down syndrome are unable to handle everything on their own. Often, other adults need to take on most of the work. So, when an adult with Down syndrome really thinks about all the work involved in having a child, he or she usually agrees that having a baby is not for them!

If your brother or sister decides against having a baby, he or she can still enjoy being around little ones. He or she can help out with nieces and nephews—taking them on outings, helping to babysit, and buying presents for them. Some adults with Down syndrome choose to help out in childcare settings or the nursery school at their place of worship.

Will my brother be able to live on his own when he is an adult?

Adults with Down syndrome have many different options for living arrangements. Some might choose to live with family members. Others might live in a "group home" with roommates who might or might not have disabilities, and some might choose to live independently in their own apartment or house. Regardless of where they choose to live, most adults with Down syndrome will require some assistance with daily activities.

> Regardless of where they choose to live, most adults with Down syndrome will require some assistance with daily activities.

Many communities have resources available to help adults with disabilities live independently. Some adults who live in group homes have aides or workers who visit on a regular basis to provide assistance with cooking, money management, taking medications, and transportation. Other times, family members might choose to pay for such services in order to allow a person with Down syndrome to live as independently as possible. How much support adults with Down syndrome need depends on how much they are able to do on their own.

You might be asking yourself: will my brother with Down syndrome need to live with me when my parents are older or no longer living? In some families, everyone agrees that the best living arrangement for a person with Down syndrome is with a close relation such as a brother, sister, or cousin. This kind of a decision is not usually made until all the siblings are adults.

However, as we pointed out above, this certainly is not the only option for your brother as he gets older. If you are concerned about this situation, consider thinking about the following:

- If your brother is a teenager or older, your parents will probably have a discussion with him about his goals for the future. He might or might not have an idea about where he would like to live—in fact, he may never have thought about living anywhere other than home. But, you might very well be surprised that he has his own opinions about the matter!

- Have a conversation with your parents about their expectations for your brother as he gets older. Have they made plans for his future? Where do they envision him living as they get older or are no longer living? They might already have some plans in place that they can share with you. When parents have plans arranged well in advance, siblings are often relieved that they don't have to make all the future decisions.

- If living independently with or without a support system is not an option for your brother, ask your parents what expectations they have for you in your brother's future. Share with them your honest feelings about whether you can see your brother moving in with you one day (and it is okay if you can't). You might find that your feelings change as you get older, but expressing your honest opinions with your parents can help them make practical plans for your brother's future. Many parents hope that siblings remain involved enough that they will, at least, make sure that their brother with Down syndrome is happy, safe, and has enough money. This does not necessarily mean you need to live with him or take care of all his needs.

Will my sister ever be able to drive a car?

We all have hopes and dreams, but there are some life milestones that often seem necessary along the road to growing up: driving a car, going to college, getting married, having children. Driving a car is often the first major milestone your sister will be anxious to accomplish. But it's also a difficult one. Not only does she have to pass a written driving test about the rules of the road, she has to be able to actually drive the car! The driver needs to know how to turn on the car, drive forward and in reverse, and operate the lights and the windshield wipers. She needs to drive the correct speed, stop at lights, read signs, and be able to react quickly when a dog runs across the street.

> People with Down syndrome often react more slowly in a dangerous situation.

People with Down syndrome often react more slowly in a dangerous situation. They may also have difficulty doing two things at once—like staying at the correct speed and keeping the car on the right side of the line. For this reason, most people with Down syndrome do not drive cars on their own. In some rare cases, however, driving a car may be a more realistic goal if you live in a rural area with little traffic and straight, two-lane roads.

If your sister wants to and is able to drive a car, she should go for it! But, if she is not able to, she should begin to think about how she can get where she needs to go by using other means of transportation.

If driving a car is your sister's dream, and you don't think this is a possibility for her, check out pages 114-15 for some thoughts on how to approach this topic with her. Driving centers and rehabilitation hospitals often have virtual driving situations where your sister can be evaluated to see if she actually has the skills needed to drive.

What kind of jobs can my sister with Down syndrome get when she is older?

Your sister can and should pursue any number of jobs. People with Down syndrome are employed in lots of ways: as teachers' aides, mailroom delivery persons, office assistants, cleaning staff, grocery store baggers, stockroom clerks, restaurant workers, musicians, and actors, just to name a few.

When your sister begins to think about job possibilities, she should consider the following ideas with your family:

■ **Is the job one that she would enjoy?** We all work better when we are enthusiastic about the task. Finding a job that is interesting will be key to your sister's success. Many times, people with Down syndrome are given jobs that are extremely boring or tiring. They can quickly lose interest (or fall asleep at the job), and then be asked to find another source of employment. On the other hand, these simpler jobs might be most enjoyable for your sister if she likes to work at her own pace and with minimal pressure.

> Finding a job that is interesting will be key to your sister's success.

■ **Does the job utilize her talents?** Your sister can probably do a lot of things really well (such as organizing), but she might have trouble with other tasks (such as counting money). Finding a job that maximizes her talents and minimizes her trouble areas will be another important element of her future success. For example, your sister might enjoy restocking novels at a bookstore (if she likes organizing), but she might not enjoy being the store's cashier (if she has trouble handling money).

■ **Who else will be working with your sister?** Your sister probably has a good idea of the types of settings she likes best. Does she prefer to be around people with disabilities, or would she like to work with people who primarily do not have disabilities? Does she prefer to work at a place with a lot of people, or does she like to work in a smaller setting with just a few coworkers? Her choice might stem from the educational environment that she is used to, as we discussed in Chapter 2. Many jobs are created just for groups of people with disabilities. Other jobs are in settings where people with and without disabilities interact. It will be important to pick a job that has the environment your sister is comfortable with and wants.

■ **Does your sister want to be paid for her work?** Some people with Down syndrome want to get paid just like anyone else who works in the same job. Others do not care if they are paid and are happy to work on a volunteer basis. Some might have restrictions on how much they can get paid, due to federal requirements dealing with their Social Security and medical insurance (see next question). Determining how important a paycheck is for your sister will be helpful in deciding which jobs are best for her.

■ **Will your sister need support on the job?** Many adults with Down syndrome need some coaching during the first couple of weeks or months so that they can learn to do their job as well as they possibly can. New jobs can sometimes be daunting with so many new things to learn! If your sister will need some support, it will be important to find out whether another employee can provide that support and training. Alternatively, a "job coach" might be available from the community to help your sister. "Job coaches" are people who are trained to help people with disabilities learn how to do their jobs well.

■ **How will your sister get to the job?** Transportation is often-times a barrier for people with Down syndrome seeking employment. If your sister needs to walk to work, that might limit her options. But your family might be able to drive her, or explore public transportation, carpooling, or the use of taxi service.

If your sister is interested, she will almost certainly be able to be employed and contribute in very meaningful ways to her community.

I keep hearing my parents talking about a Social Security check for my brother. What does this refer to?

In the U.S., when people with Down syndrome turn 18 years old, they can be eligible to receive extra income from a governmental source called Supplemental Security Income (SSI). SSI was established, in part, to help people with disabilities make enough money to live. The government recognized that many adults with disabilities do not earn enough money through jobs, so the government gives extra money, for free, to qualified people so that they can pay for necessities.

If your brother is over 18 and receiving a "Social Security check," he is probably getting a check through the SSI program. This check can range anywhere from $0 to $600, depending on how much money your brother makes in his job. In short, the more money your brother makes on his own, the less money the government feels they should give him. A recent study has shown that the average adult with Down syndrome earns $410 each month in job wages and receives $487 in SSI benefits.

Advocacy organizations such as the National Down Syndrome Society (NDSS) and the National Down Syndrome Congress (NDSC) believe that there are many ways to improve SSI.

Supplemental Security Income was established, in part, to help people with disabilities make enough money to live.

These organizations and many families feel that the current system limits, rather than supports, employment opportunities for people with Down syndrome. Many adults with Down syndrome must ask a crucial question: "How much money can I earn at my job without losing my SSI payments?" In today's society, when adults with Down syndrome are achieving and maintaining new levels of success in the workplace, they must also balance a careful income game—earning too much might disqualify them from critical SSI benefits.

If you have more questions about SSI payments, ask your parents, as they are likely familiar with how this might work for your brother.

As my sister gets older, what if she cannot master the things that most adults do?

Let's talk about "life trophies." Some people judge their success by the amount of money in their bank accounts, the number of polished cars in their garage, or the number of diamonds sparkling on their fingers. These are their "life trophies," accomplishments that make them feel proud and important. Some other people, however, judge their worth by the lasting marks that they have made on their communities and the people that they have touched in their lifetime. Their "life trophies" are different, aren't they? These people find success—and happiness—in outward actions, ways in which they have influenced their neighbors and strangers.

What your sister will begin to teach you—if she hasn't done so already—is that life can be judged by this different set of criteria: the number of people she has made laugh, the service she has provided to the community, the misperceptions that she has changed in her lifetime.

> Find reasons to celebrate your sibling's everyday successes, no matter how big or small.

So, what about driving a car? Going to college? Getting married? Having children? All of these activities, as we discussed in this chapter, are possible for some people with Down syndrome, but it does not mean that they are all the right options for your sister. What is even more important to remember is that none of these accomplishments are even necessary to make your sister important. Her contributions to your family, her community, and society, in general, can be just as great—if not greater—than those of people who do drive, go to college, get married, and have children. Find reasons to celebrate your sibling's everyday successes, no matter how big or small.

SUMMARY POINTS

- People with Down syndrome can and do fall in love. Dating, however, is often complicated by lack of transportation or money. You or your parents might be able to help your sibling out by driving him to his date or arranging a double date.

- Some people with Down syndrome do get married. Choosing to remain single, however, does not make a person any less important.

- The fertility rates in men and women with Down syndrome are lower than in adults without Down syndrome. But people with Down syndrome can have babies both with and without Down syndrome. The number who do, however, is very small.

- Adults with Down syndrome have many different options for living arrangements. Some continue to live with their parents or siblings; others live with or without roommates in their own place, usually with some support staff providing assistance with daily living. Still others live in a group home with a few other adults with disabilities.

- When pursuing a job, your sibling should take into account her own personal interests, whether she wants to get paid, what types of on-site support services are available, who she will work with, and how she will get to and from work.

- When people with Down syndrome turn 18 years old, they can be eligible to receive extra income from a governmental source called Supplemental Security Income (SSI). Since many adults with disabilities do not earn enough money through their jobs, the government gives them this extra money, for free, so that they can pay for necessities.

9 ROAD SIGNS :
local and national resources

If you've found this book helpful, you might be interested in exploring additional opportunities to connect with brothers and sisters who have siblings with Down syndrome. The resources in this chapter might help you meet other siblings face-to-face right in your own community. Or, through listservs, books, and newsletters, you might find additional information and support to help you answer questions and handle difficult moments in your everyday life.

Are there any newsletters just for brothers and sisters of individuals with Down syndrome?

As of the printing of this book, there are no newsletters that we know of just for brothers and sisters of individuals with Down syndrome. There are, however, online newsletters available for siblings of people with any type of disability. Family Resource Associates, a small agency in New Jersey working with individuals with disabilities and their families, has produced many newsletters for siblings. *For Siblings Only* is designed for children aged 4 to 9, and *Sibling Forum* targets students aged 10 to 19. Each issue provides information on different disabilities, library resources, and a discussion of feelings and concerns. Past newsletters can be downloaded, for free, at www.frainc.org.

Band of Angels Foundation, a publishing and outreach organization for Down syndrome, frequently posts articles on its web page that are specifically for brothers and sisters who have siblings with Down syndrome. Check it out at www.bandofangels.com.

Are there any listservs just for siblings that I could sign up for?

Listservs are emails that are sent to a "list" of people, all at once. Generally, listservs are devoted to a particular topic. Some are open to anyone in the world who has an interest in that topic; others require that a moderator approve your membership. Listserv participants can just read messages and questions submitted by others, or they can ask their own questions, share stories, and respond to others people's messages.

You can find listservs for siblings who have brothers and sisters with many different types of disabilities at www.siblingsupport.org. There is a listserv for younger brothers and sisters called SibKids and one for adult brothers and sisters called SibNet.

As of the printing of this book, we do not know of any specific listservs or online chat rooms specifically for brothers and sisters who have siblings with Down syndrome.

Where can I sign up for a sibling group for brothers and sisters of individuals with Down syndrome?

The National Down Syndrome Congress (NDSC) has a national convention once a year for families who have individuals with Down syndrome. As part of these conferences, there are workshops designed just for brothers and sisters. That's right—these sessions are just for you! No parents. No siblings. In a safe and confidential setting, you can meet and share your ideas—and frustrations—with other brothers and sisters. If your family is considering attending one of these conferences, usually held in the summer, why not go along and take advantage of the sibling program? For more information on when the next conference will be, go to the NDSC's web page at www.ndsccenter.org.

Sibling workshops may also be part of regional, state-wide, or local conferences on Down syndrome. Additionally, some local agencies that provide services to individuals with Down syndrome and other disabilities, like the Arc, might host sibling groups. Even if they do not run sibling programs, they might have information on workshops or conferences happening in your area, perhaps even at your area hospital. Your parents are probably on the mailing list for local agencies and conferences. Ask your parents if they have further information on sibling groups. If not, you or someone in your family can contact the agency or Down syndrome group in your area and ask if they will be sponsoring a sibling workshop any time soon.

Still another way to locate a sibling group near you is to visit www.siblingsupport.org. While the group will most likely include brothers and sisters whose siblings have disabilities other than Down syndrome, you'll find you have plenty in common with just about all of them!

What are some organizations about Down syndrome?

Printed below are the major national Down syndrome organizations. Be sure to check out their web pages where you can find more information about what they do.

National Down Syndrome Congress (NDSC)
1370 Center Drive, Suite 102
Atlanta, GA 30338
(800) 232-6372
www.ndsccenter.org
info@ndsccenter.org

National Down Syndrome Society (NDSS)
666 Broadway
New York, NY 10012
(800) 221-4602
www.ndss.org
info@ndss.org

Down Syndrome Research and Treatment Foundation (DSRTF)
755 Page Mill Road, Suite A200
Palo Alto, CA 94304
(650) 468-1668
www.dsrtf.org
dsrtf@dsrft.org

Canadian Down Syndrome Society (CDSS)
811 – 14 Street NW
Calgary, Alberta
72N 2A4
Canada
(800) 883-5608
www.cdss.ca
info@cdss.ca

There are also numerous regional, state, and local Down syndrome organizations. You can find the organization that is nearest you by searching for local resources on the website of the NDSS at www.ndss.org.

What are some good books for finding general information about Down syndrome?

For an up-to-date list of good books on Down syndrome, go to www.ndsccenter.org. Most of you might be interested in taking a look at one or two of them. Here is a just a sample of some books; descriptions are borrowed from the NDSC with permission:

Common Threads: Celebrating Life with Down Syndrome by
Brian Skotko and Cynthia Kidder. Rochester Hills, MI:
Band of Angels Press, 2001.
(www.bandofangels.com, 800-963-2237)
Essays and photographs celebrate inspirational accomplishments of people with Down syndrome. This is a great book for a reader of any age to enjoy.

Babies with Down Syndrome: A New Parent's Guide (3rd Edition) edited by Susan J. Skallerup. Bethesda, MD: Woodbine House, 2008. (www.woodbinehouse.com, 800-843-7323)

This is a complete guide written for new parents, but you might find some of the information on medical issues, genetics, or early intervention helpful.

Adolescents with Down Syndrome: Toward a More Fulfilling Life
edited by Siegfried Pueschel and Maria Sustrova. Baltimore, MD: Brookes Publishing, 1997.
(www.pbrookes.com, 800-638-3775)
If you are interested in learning more about teens with Down syndrome, this is a good book for you.

Adults with Down Syndrome by Siegfried Pueschel. Baltimore, MD: Brookes Publishing, 2006.
(www.pbrookes.com, 800-638-3775)
Want to learn more about what adulthood is like for people with Down syndrome? Then be sure to check this book out. The book combines information written by professionals who work with adults with Down syndrome along with personal essays by self-advocates. Topics include medical and mental health, employment, post-secondary education, social relationships, and living arrangements.

A Special Kind of Hero: Chris Burke's Own Story by Chris Burke and Jo Beth McDaniel. New York, NY: Bantam Doubleday Dell, 1991. (www.randomhouse.com/bantamdell)
The star of the TV show "Life Goes On" tells his remarkable story and the pursuit of his "impossible dreams."

Count Us In: Growing Up with Down Syndrome (2nd Edition) by Jason Kingsley and Mitchell Levitz. New York, NY: Harcourt Brace, 2007. (www.harcourtbooks.com, 212-592-1000)
A unique and powerful book of conversations with two young men with Down syndrome.

What are some good books on siblings' issues about Down syndrome?

The following books are for brothers and sisters who have siblings with disabilities, but not Down syndrome in particular. This list was borrowed, with permission, from the National Down Syndrome Congress. You can find the most updated list at www.ndsccenter.org.

Views from Our Shoes: Growing Up With a Brother or Sister with Special Needs by Donald Meyer. Bethesda, MD: Woodbine House, 1997. (www.woodbinehouse.com, 800-843-7323)
   A collection of essays by children and young adults who have a sibling with special needs.

Living with a Brother or Sister with Special Needs: A Book for Sibs by Donald Meyer and Patricia Vadasy. Seattle, WA: University of Washington Press, 1996. (www.washington.edu/uwpress, 800-441-4115)
   In easy-to-understand terms, discusses specific disabilities and the intense emotions brothers and sisters experience.

The Sibling Slam Book: What it's REALLY Like to Have a Brother or Sister with Special Needs edited by Donald Meyer. Bethesda, MD: Woodbine House, 2005. (www.woodbinehouse.com, 800-843-7323)
   The thoughts and feelings of 80 teen siblings from around the world are included in the answers to 54 posed questions.

You might also be interested in fictional books featuring siblings and their brothers or sisters with Down syndrome or other disabilities. The librarian at your local library might be of help in locating some titles. The list below offers a few examples:

Radiance Descending by Paula Fox. New York: Bantam Doubleday Dell Books for Young Readers, 1997.
Paul is an eleven-year-old who has a brother with Down
syndrome, four years younger (currently out-of-print but available at some libraries).

My Sister Annie by Bill Dodds. Nonesdale, PA: Boyds Mill
Press, 1993.
Charlie is an eleven-year-old whose older sister has Down
syndrome and tends to embarrass him with his friends.

My Brother is a World Class Pain by Michael Gordon. DeWitt,
NY: GSI Publications, 1992.
This book describes life in a family with someone with at-
tention deficit hyperactivity disorder (ADHD).

A few novels written for young adults and adults also have
characters with disabilities. You might find a book, like one of
the two mentioned here, of interest as well.

The Memory Keeper's Daughter by Kim Edwards. New York,
NY: Viking, 2005.
On a wintery day in 1964, a father decides to give his baby
with Down syndrome away while his wife recovers from the
labor. He tells her that the baby died in pregnancy. This novel
follows Phoebe, the baby with Down syndrome who grows up,
and her mother who never knew she lived.

The Curious Incident of the Dog in the Night-time by Mark Had-
don. New York, NY: Vintage Books, 2002.
Written from the viewpoint of Christopher, a young boy
with autism, this book takes you on a mystery to unlock who
killed a neighbor's dog.

How can I stay up to date on breaking news about Down syndrome?

People with Down syndrome are appearing in the news all of the time. To stay current on the latest news—or advances in research—here are two easy tips:

1. Go to www.google.com and click around until you find the option of Google Alerts. Google will search all for news on topics that you are interested in and email you the results as often as you want. If you type "Down syndrome," you can have a summary of all of the articles on Down syndrome in the news e-mailed to you every day or every week.

2. Go to www.patriciaebauer.com. This web page is maintained by a journalist who is also the mother of a daughter with Down syndrome. Every day, she posts many of the news articles on people with disabilities that appear in national and international media. Here you can read about the latest controversies, newest discoveries, and personal triumphs that are being discussed in newspapers, radios, and televisions across the country.

INDEX

About the Authors:

Brian Skotko, M.D., M.P.P., a physician at Children's Hospital Boston and Boston Medical Center, has dedicated his professional energies toward children with cognitive and developmental disabilities. He is a national speaker whose research has been featured in *The Wall Street Journal, The New York Times, The Washington Post, The L.A. Times,* NPR's On Point, and ABC's Good Morning America. In 2001 he co-authored the national award-winning book, *Common Threads: Celebrating Life with Down Syndrome.* He has two adult sisters, one of whom has Down syndrome.

Susan Levine, M.A., C.S.W., is a co-founder and social worker at Family Resource Associates, Inc., a private, nonprofit agency in central New Jersey. She has conducted support programs for parents and siblings of children with differing abilities for the past 30 years. She has presented on the needs of siblings at national and regional conferences on Down syndrome, spina bifida, and Rett syndrome, as well as for New Jersey school system parent groups. Additionally, she writes quarterly newsletters for brothers and sisters.

About the Illustrator:

Catie Liken, an artist with a master's degree in architecture, developed her design and illustration skills while working with architectural rendering and representation. Her original designs have been included in the *Columbia Abstract,* Columbia University's yearly publication featuring the top work produced at the school. She is currently working in New York City at a commercial post-production and special effects house. More of her work can be viewed on her website, www.catieliken.com.